Praise for *The Art of Lucid Dreaming*

"With a panoramic collection of lucid dream techniques, *The Art of Lucid Dreaming* helps dreamers enter, enhance, and prolong their lucid dream states, and inspires those who wish to develop an even deeper practice of blissful dreaming."

—Anna-Karin Bjorklund, author of *The Dream Alchemist*

"Dr. Clare Johnson is a masterful guide to the exploration of this creative and cosmic state of consciousness known as lucid dreaming. A delightful must-read!"

—Robert Hoss, author/editor of *Dreams that Change Our Lives*

"There is no better lucid dreaming teacher than Dr. Clare R. Johnson. The information and exercises provided in this book will be life changing."

—Jean Campbell, editor of *DreamTime*

"[A] bonanza of useful information that will save the aspiring lucid dreamer a huge amount of time in achieving their goal."

—Dr. Keith Hearne, pioneering scientist who provided the first proof of lucid dreaming and author of *The Dream Machine*

"There is nothing like *The Art of Lucid Dreaming*—the tools contained within, including the Lucidity Quiz, are creative and effective … If you've been praying to experience your first lucid dream, or desiring many more, this book will guide you toward your goal, with a dash of humor, in the most individualized way possible."

—Kimberly R. Mascaro, PhD, author of *Extraordinary Dreams* and the blog Consciouschimera.com

"*The Art of Lucid Dreaming* wins the award for the most practical guide to lucid dreaming ever! There's no fluff, just the practices and the mindsets that lead to a more conscious dream life … Highly recommended for new and advanced lucid dreamers alike!"

—Ryan Hurd, author of *Lucid Immersion Guidebook* and founder of DreamStudies.org

"Dr. Clare Johnson provides proven strategies that will help beginners unlock their capacity to experience lucid dreams and assist advanced lucid dreamers in exploring new frontiers. Regardless of one's prior experience with lucid dreaming, this book should be on every dream explorer's bookshelf."

—Scott Sparrow, EdD, author of *Lucid Dreaming*

"Practical, streamlined, fun, and highly effective, [this] is the perfect introductory manual for those students of oneironautics who are eager to start lucid dreaming tonight, as well as those veteran lucid dreamers who could use some valuable new tips … Beautifully written and highly recommended!"

—David Jay Brown, author of *Dreaming Wide Awake*

"Whether you want to get started on the subject or you are an experienced lucid dreamer, this book will gently accompany you so that you can design your own personalized strategy, guided by Dr. Johnson's experienced, clear and playful writing, her Lucidity Quiz, and unique lucidity programs … All in all, a true gift."

—Jordi Borràs-García, psychologist and
founder of www.mondesomnis.com

"For anyone who is looking to add new life to their dream experience, this is the book for you. Dr. Johnson provides structured, easy-to-read, and vibrant guidance to help you create your personal approach for your journey into and through the world of lucid dreaming."

—Robert P. Gongloff, author of *Dream
Exploration: A New Approach*

"An excellent practical guide into the marvellous world of lucid dreaming: inspiring, resourceful and fun to read. *The Art of Lucid Dreaming* will help you to develop your own unique approach in unlocking your ability to lucid dream and will empower you with dozens of techniques and exercises to become lucid, stay lucid, and reach the heights and depths of this wondrous state of consciousness."

—Dr. Tadas Stumbrys, psychologist
and lucid dream researcher

the *Art* of
LUCID
DREAMING

About the Author

Clare R. Johnson, PhD, is president and CEO of the world's biggest dream organisation, the International Association for the Study of Dreams (IASD). A lifelong, frequent lucid dreamer, Clare has more than forty years of personal lucid dream experience and in 2007 became the first person in the world to do a PhD on lucid dreaming as a creative writing tool. She has researched lucid dreaming  for twenty-five years, and for the past fifteen years she has taught practical courses on how to access the deep creative and healing potential of the unconscious.

Clare is the author of the acclaimed book *Llewellyn's Complete Book of Lucid Dreaming: A Comprehensive Guide to Promote Creativity, Overcome Sleep Disturbances & Enhance Health and Wellness*. Clare's work on lucid dreaming has been featured in documentaries, magazines, anthologies, national radio shows, podcasts, and television. She regularly speaks at international venues on topics as diverse as lucid dreams for the dying, sleep disturbances, transformative lucidity techniques, and nightmare solutions.

A novelist, prize-winning short story writer, and poet, Clare is the author of two lucid-dream-inspired novels (as Clare Jay). *Breathing in Colour* looks at how lucid dreaming can heal trauma, and *Dreamrunner* explores lucidity as a potential cure for violent moving nightmares. A passionate advocate of lucid dreaming and waking dreamwork as a way to empower children, Clare co-edited a book on children's dreams and nightmares: *Sleep Monsters & Superheroes: Empowering Children through Creative Dreamplay*. Her nonfiction book *Dream Therapy: Dream Your Way to Health and Happiness* (US title is *Mindful Dreaming*) explores the transformative effect that dreamwork can have on our lives.

You may feel inspired to join Clare on her lucid dreaming retreats. These usually have a beautiful ocean setting, and the creative, healing, wild, and spiritual aspects of lucidity are explored in a small group. For more information, email deepluciddreaming@gmail.com.

Clare is the creator of www.DeepLucidDreaming.com, where she can be contacted for advice on lucid dreams and nightmares.

the *Art* of LUCID DREAMING

Over 60 Powerful Practices *to* Help *you* Wake Up *in your* Dreams

CLARE R. JOHNSON, PhD

Llewellyn Publications
Woodbury, Minnesota

FIRST EDITION
Third Printing, 2021

Book design by Samantha Penn
Cover design by Shira Atakpu

Llewellyn Publications is a registered trademark of Llewellyn Worldwide Ltd.

Library of Congress Cataloging-in-Publication Data
Names: Johnson, Clare R., author.
Title: The art of lucid dreaming : over 60 powerful practices to help you
    wake up in your dreams / Clare R. Johnson, PhD.
Description: First edition. | Woodbury, Minnesota : Llewellyn Worldwide,
    Ltd, 2020. | Includes bibliographical references and index.
Identifiers: LCCN 2019051422 (print) | LCCN 2019051423 (ebook) | ISBN
    9780738762654 | ISBN 9780738762975 (ebook)
Subjects: LCSH: Lucid dreams.
Classification: LCC BF1099.L82 J638 2020 (print) | LCC BF1099.L82 (ebook)
    | DDC 154.6/3—dc23
LC record available at https://lccn.loc.gov/2019051422
LC ebook record available at https://lccn.loc.gov/2019051423

Llewellyn Publications
A Division of Llewellyn Worldwide Ltd.
2143 Wooddale Drive
Woodbury, MN 55125-2989
www.llewellyn.com

Printed in the United States of America

Other Books by Clare R. Johnson, PhD

Breathing in Colour

Dreamrunner

*Sleep Monsters & Superheroes: Empowering
Children through Creative Dreamplay* (Coedited)

*Llewellyn's Complete Book of Lucid Dreaming:
A Comprehensive Guide to Promote Creativity, Overcome
Sleep Disturbances & Enhance Health and Wellness*

*Dream Therapy: Dream Your Way to Health
and Happiness* (US title: *Mindful Dreaming*)

To Dr. Keith Hearne, for his pioneering work in the field of lucid dreaming

Contents

Part One
Getting Lucid: How to
Wake Up in Your Dreams

Part Two
Staying Lucid: How to Have Longer,
More Satisfying Lucid Dreams

Part Three
Best Techniques for
Guiding Lucid Dreams

Practices

Chapter 3: Relax Your Way Into Lucid Dreaming

Chapter 4: Create Your Unique Lucidity Programme

Part Two
Staying Lucid: How to Have Longer,
More Satisfying Lucid Dreams

Chapter 5: Powerful Practices for Longer Lucid Dreams

Chapter 6: Train Your Mind to
Keep on Lucid Dreaming

Part Three
Best Techniques for
Guiding Lucid Dreams

Disclaimer

This book offers techniques for working with lucid dreams. It is not a substitute for psychological counselling or medical advice. If you have any physical or mental health concerns, you must consult your doctor or other medical practitioner. The author assumes no responsibility or liability for the actions of the reader.

Acknowledgments

I'm grateful to the intrepid lucid dreamers who openly share enchanting lucid dreams and bone-chilling nightmares with me in workshops and on lucid dreaming retreats, and all those who write to me. I feel honoured to share their journey into the thrilling world of sleep and dreams.

Huge thanks to Angela Wix and the rest of the multi-talented team at Llewellyn Worldwide for their care and excellence.

My love and thanks go to Markus and Yasmin for bringing me light and laughter and supporting my adventure into a new lucid dreaming book.

Introduction

Imagine yourself curled up in your warm bed, fast asleep. From the outside, you may appear inactive, but you are dreaming hard and fast, swept up in a world of vivid imagery and strong emotions, where gravity has no set rules and pigs might indeed fly. Your eyes flicker under your eyelids but you can't feel your body: you are lost to the waking world.

In your dream, you are strolling alongside a river when a tiger with rippling muscles and velvety stripes bounds into your path. For a split second you stare into its glowing eyes. Your body kicks into a fear reaction: adrenaline pumps, your heart jumps, you break into a terrified sweat. The tiger snarls and you know it's about to spring you.

Then you understand the truth of the situation—you are *dreaming*! Yes—this is a *dream* tiger, and no matter what happens next, you know that afterwards you will wake up safely in your bed with no torn flesh or mauled limbs.

Relief flows through you, along with the marvellous clarity of knowing that you are "awake inside a dream." Your vision sharpens, your heart slows … and your fear dissolves. You look in wonder at this incredibly realistic tiger, and to your amazement it lowers its massive head and takes a docile step towards you. Awed, you reach out and stroke its warm fur. Your hand buzzes with orange dream tiger energy and it feels fantastic.

This is lucid dreaming.

A lucid dream is when we *know* that we are dreaming, while we are dreaming. We activate our waking awareness in a dream, without actually waking up.

"How Do I Get Lucid in My Dreams?"

This is the number one question I hear from a wide range of people: from artists looking to tap into the original creativity of lucid dreaming, to journalists writing their first article on this topic, to people from all professions excited by the idea that *there is more to sleep than just sleeping*! We sleep a third of our lives away. Yes, sleep is essential, healing, and downright marvellous, but when we spend the entire night unconscious and don't even recall our dreams, we are looking at years and years of our life lost in oblivion.

A full six years of our life is spent dreaming, with an estimated 2,000 dreams each per year—where do these experiences vanish to? When we wake up inside our dreams, we can interact consciously with the fantastic creativity of our dreaming mind. We can extend and enhance our life experience by bringing our lucid awareness to the symbolic stories that unfold night after night as we sleep. Just some of the experiences that lucid dreamers report include: creating a new planet; having sex with someone super-desirable; befriending wild animals; flying low over the ocean; transforming into a dragon or an eagle; surfing down black holes; experimenting with being a different gender; turning into a giant and becoming super-strong; dying in different ways; performing magical tricks such as levitating objects or disappearing atom by atom; examining the tiny details of the dream world; asking profound questions about the nature of reality and receiving responses; directing healing energy to themselves or others; communicating with dream figures; and dissolving into blissful light.

It's no wonder the question, "How do I get lucid?" becomes urgent when we grasp how enriching and exciting lucid dreaming can be. This book introduces original practices that I've created myself and tested in interactive workshops and mentoring schemes over the years with transformative results. It also includes the most effective lucidity practices that I have encountered through decades of personal experimentation, research, and through teaching lucid dreaming. The plan is to give you tools to develop your own tailor-made practice by engaging imaginatively with these techniques and shaping them to suit you personally depending on your dreamer /sleeper type.

A key concept in this book is that any lucid dreaming technique can be seen as a recipe that you can tinker with to suit your individual taste. When we interact playfully and creatively with lucid dreaming techniques, we raise our overall lucid awareness and increase our chances of successfully getting lucid. Within the pages of this book, you'll find many practices to help you actively develop your own unique range of techniques for getting and staying lucid.

There will always be people along the way with a tendency to mystify lucid dreaming. But while it does open a mysterious and truly wonderful world to us, there is nothing mysterious about having lucid dreams. This is an entirely normal thing! Kids can do it, old people can do it, and so can everybody in between. I had my first flash of dream lucidity when I was three, and I know an octogenarian who has been lucid dreaming for six decades. Don't believe anyone who says lucid dreaming is only for Tibetan Buddhist monks, shamans, advanced meditators, or for people who have done a particular training programme. What nonsense! You are ready to get lucid at any moment, in waking life and in dreams. All anyone else can offer is their own perspective and their version of which steps to take, but ultimately you are the only one who can take these steps for yourself.

Lucid dreaming is for everyone and I encourage you to make your own discoveries about this fascinating state of consciousness that is accessible to all of us. It's good to read widely on the subject, explore different authors and their individual paths into lucid dreaming, and always look to your own experience for your own "answers" about lucid dreaming. Find out for yourself! There's nothing stopping you. When we imagine obstacles, we create them. Obstacles to lucidity are only as strong as we allow them to be. We'll be examining the incredible power of belief as we go deeper into lucid dreaming, as well as considering the power of our thoughts to shape our reality… and guide our dreams.

Often people feel impatient, hoping that once they find *the* simple lucid dreaming induction technique they're looking for, they'll be "in" and won't need to work on developing skills such as mental clarity and critical thinking. That's understandable—lucid dreaming is so wonderful and full of potential, of course we want to get on with it! Yet even if we get lucid in a dream, it's likely to be a frustratingly brief experience if we don't cultivate basic lucidity skills. Guiding the dream becomes so much simpler when we work with the powerful tools of intent, clarity, and expectation, so this book is filled with practices that help you to naturally develop these core skills as you go along.

Back when I was first learning to lucid dream at will, I would have leaped for joy to find a book with practical tips on how to increase my lucid dreaming frequency and successfully have longer lucid dreams. That's why I've written this book—I hope it will be the most practical lucid dreaming induction guide you could need. *The Art of Lucid Dreaming* is filled with powerful practices for lucid dreaming. Its goal is to help you to get lucid, increase the frequency of your lucid dreams, stay lucid for longer, and successfully navigate the exhilarating world of lucid dreaming.

How Did I Get into Lucid Dreaming?

When I was three years old, I briefly became lucid in a dream in which I was drowning in a turquoise swimming pool. I realised I could either stay in the dream and drown, or wake up. I chose to wake up from that dream, but enjoyed an incredibly vivid and active dream life throughout my childhood. I had recurring lucid dreams of flying over the house and finding magical books filled with wisdom, mingled with less lovely lucid nightmares of getting all tangled up in buzzing overhead power lines. Since my family had zero interest in dreams, I was told that "dreams are not real," which always bemused me since my dreams were as real as real could be!

At Lancaster University in the UK, I began a serious exploration of lucid dreaming and taught myself to lucid dream at will, using many of the techniques that appear in this book. In 1995 I did undergraduate work on lucid dreams. Later on, I embarked on doctoral research into lucid dreaming with the University of Leeds, UK,[1] and discovered the International Association for the Study of Dreams (IASD), the world's biggest dream organisation. Lucid dreaming was considered a fringe topic by most academics back then, but IASD was wonderfully supportive of my research. I went to my first IASD dream conference in Copenhagen in 2004 and was blown away—finally, I met hundreds of people who all valued dreams as much as I did!

It was a revelation and a huge boost as I faced resistance from sceptical academics who seemed to suspect that lucid dreaming wasn't really possible, and therefore was not a suitable topic for doctoral research. Of course, lucid dreaming has been a scientifically proved phenomenon of sleep ever since Dr. Keith Hearne's ground-breaking experiments in 1975,[2] so science was on my side.

These days, I'm honoured to be President and CEO of the International Association for the Study of Dreams. I became the first person in the world to do a PhD on lucid dreaming as a creative writing tool. I've clocked up more than forty years of personal exploration into lucid dreaming as a lifelong, frequent lucid dreamer, and I've researched lucid dreaming for almost twenty-five years. For the past fifteen years I've taught practical courses on how to access the creative, healing, and transformative potential of the unconscious. You could say that lucid dreaming is my life! (Don't worry, I do have other interests too.) Since 2009 I've had five dream books published and I'll mention them briefly so you can see how different they are from each other.

My two lucid-dream-inspired novels (as Clare Jay) are *Dreamrunner*, which looks at the impact of a violent sleep disorder on one family, and *Breathing in Colour*, which explores how lucid dreaming can help resolve trauma. I've also co-edited a book on how to empower children with their dreams and nightmares: *Sleep Monsters & Superheroes*.

My first non-fiction book, *Dream Therapy* (*Mindful Dreaming* is the US title), explores how we can draw on the wisdom of dreams every night to transform our lives for the better. Its focus is on mindful sleep and waking dreamwork, and it highlights the healing potential of "Lucid Dreamplay"—my range

---

1. Johnson, "The Role of Lucid Dreaming in the Process of Creative Writing."
2. Hearne, "Lucid Dreams: An Electro-Physiological and Psychological Study."

of key dreamworking tools—and the transformative effect these can have on our lives.

Llewellyn's Complete Book of Lucid Dreaming is huge in scope, combining cutting-edge science, psychology, practical techniques, and academic studies with a very deep approach to lucid dreaming, as it explores healing, sexual dreams, grief, sleep disturbances, meditation, creativity, death, and transcendent lucid states … and that's just for starters. It's a tome!

What's in This Book?

In comparison, *The Art of Lucid Dreaming* is a super-practical, quick, and easy how-to guide packed with powerful practices and lucidity programmes. It focuses on lucid dreaming induction and stabilisation techniques, as well as how to guide dreams with the power of thoughts and expectations. This book does what other lucid dreaming books don't do—it gets you focused on yourself as a highly individual sleeper and dreamer and enables you to leapfrog ahead to the techniques that are most likely to be effective for you.

The Lucidity Quiz in chapter 4 is a cornerstone of the book. It encourages you to identify the kind of sleeper and dreamer you are, and you'll then get clarity on how to mix and match techniques depending on your dreamer /sleeper type. I've included fifteen Lucidity Programmes for a range of different types, from the heavy sleeper to the insomniac, and the high-recall dreamer to the nightmare sufferer. These programmes are for you to combine and customise to create your own Unique Lucidity Programme to fast-track you to wake up in your dreams.

Although this book is ideal for those starting out with their lucid dreaming practice, it isn't just for beginners; experienced lucid dreamers looking to refresh their practice after a dry spell will find plenty of original practices to kick-start a new phase of lucidity. For those of you who have read my other dream books and are familiar with my core practices such as Lucid Writing and the Lucid Imaging Nightmare Solution, this book still offers a range of brand-new lucidity practices that I've created, as well as my in-depth approach to assessing your personal dreamer/sleeper type.

This latest book is deliberately non-academic because I like each of my books to offer something new, and a great number of scientific findings, academic advances, and research studies from all over the world appear in

Llewellyn's Complete Book of Lucid Dreaming. In *The Art of Lucid Dreaming*, common questions and dilemmas about lucid dreaming are answered and powerful practices are given throughout each of the three main sections: Getting Lucid, Staying Lucid, and Guiding Dreams.

This book takes you step by step through the most powerful practices for waking up in your dreams. There are a total of sixty-five practices as well as fifteen dedicated Lucidity Programmes, and in Appendix II you'll also find three examples of Unique Lucidity Programmes to help you create your own.

We'll examine how to stay lucid in the face of distractions and how to stretch our lucid mindset to enable long-lasting, frequent lucid dreams. *The Art of Lucid Dreaming* also debates the pros and cons of dream control and offers practices on topics such as how to have a successful lucid sex life, how to encourage the people in your dreams to help you get lucid, and how to fly effortlessly. We'll dive into nightmares and see how becoming lucid can help us transform bad dreams into healing gifts, and we'll look at how lucid dreaming can be a portal into transcendent experiences, as well as inspiring wild creativity and deep healing.

Enjoy the ride!

PART ONE

Getting Lucid: How to Wake Up in Your Dreams

CHAPTER 1

What Is Lucid
Dreaming?

Lucid dreams are dreams where we *know* that we are dreaming, while we are dreaming. This insight enables us to experience the gloriously rich imagery and compelling events of our dream world with full conscious awareness. We can explore the dream, go with the flow of events, actively guide the dream, and react fearlessly to scary dream situations. Lucid dreaming is a magnificent adventure open to each of us every single time we lie our heads down and sleep. Here's one lucid dream where everything changed for the better the second I knew I was dreaming:

> A huge tidal wave is hurtling towards me; a mass of towering unstoppable water. Terrified, I turn and run as fast as my legs can carry me, but I know I won't be fast enough…I glance behind me and gasp: the sun illuminates this wall of water, turning it silvery-blue and causing each tiny droplet to glimmer like diamonds. It's terrifying, but it's the most astoundingly beautiful thing I've ever seen.

Suddenly, I understand: I'm dreaming this! All my terror vanishes in a flash. As the sparkling wave barrels towards me, I leap into the air, elated. I leap so high that I land right on top of the wave, all its power beneath me. Fully lucid, with my arms outstretched, I surf this giant wave with the sun warm on my head and the taste of salt on my lips. It's so exhilarating! I surf the wave all the way down until it's foaming over green fields and I feel the ground beneath my feet.

The most common question I get asked on the subject of lucid dreaming goes along these lines: "I got lucid just the one time and it was the most awesome experience I've ever had—*how* do I do it again?"

There is no single answer because, the thing is, we're all different—we have different sleep rhythms, different lifestyles, different stressors. Some of us are visual thinkers while others are more analytical. We each enjoy different dream recall, different thought patterns, and different beliefs about the nature of reality. We even have different reasons for wanting to become lucid in our dreams. All these factors have an impact on how we respond individually to lucid dreaming induction techniques. That's why I had the idea of writing the most practical and flexible lucid dream induction book out there, to help people to discover *their own best ways* of becoming lucid in their dreams.

In this first chapter, we'll look at common questions about lucid dreaming, and how to create a lucid mindset to prime your brain to realise when you are dreaming. First of all, to whet the appetite of those of you who have yet to experience lucid dreaming, let's look at what we can do when we wake up in our dreams.

What Can We Do in Lucid Dreams?

This question might be better formulated as "what *can't* we do in lucid dreams?" There are no limits. Some people say that imagination is the only limit in lucid dreaming, but I disagree. Lucid dreams can go well beyond the bounds of the human imagination, which is why even after more than forty years of lucid dreaming, I'm not bored yet! There is no state of consciousness quite like lucid dreaming—a state where we can have wild, joyful, or transcendent experiences that we have never experienced while awake, such as flying into the sun or transforming into a raindrop.

The amazing thing is that all of this is experienced with incredible reality, clarity, and super-vivid sensations. I turned into a dolphin once and felt the torpedo strength of my body underwater, the brief flash of sunshine as I leapt powerfully over the waves, and the splash as I dove back into the water. It felt so real. A man told me that in one lucid dream, he chose to experience the wonderful sensation of being a pregnant woman and hugged the round tight drum of his belly. In lucid dreams, we can expand our life experience—we can change gender or be genderless, we can breathe underwater, shapeshift into an ant, or see what it's like to embrace a shadow man or give birth to a baby (if we're feeling brave). We can also ask the dream questions about the nature of reality, life, death, and consciousness—and receive answers from our unconscious mind. We can hug a deceased loved one and smell their familiar perfume again. We can hone physical skills, overcome phobias, have awesome sexual encounters, and learn to know ourselves from the inside out. Seriously, there are no limits!

Lucid dreaming is a fabulous tool for self-knowledge and exploring the nature of reality and conscious experience. It is also a creativity elixir—never have I seen such rampant, alive creativity as within the lucid dream state, where our thoughts, emotions, and expectations are instantly translated into vibrant streams of imagery so bright and colourful you can almost taste them on your tongue. We can learn to mine this rich creative source and bring it into our art, our writing, our current project. We can meditate in lucid dreams and experience profound interconnected oneness (if we manage not to wake up!), and lucid dreaming has massive healing potential that we are only beginning to uncover, as evidenced by psychological studies into trauma work and nightmare resolution. There is also a growing number of anecdotal reports of healing physical illness and injuries in lucid dreams.

Scientific studies[3] show that we can actually improve waking sports performance after practising in a lucid dream—people improved their dart throws, one kickboxer slowed down time to perfect a complicated kick and could do it when he woke up, while a swimmer created a pool full of honey

---

3. Schädlich, "Darts in Lucid Dreams."

to test his muscle resistance! We are still discovering the immense potential of the lucid dream state. Lucid dreaming can support and nourish us while we process the painful emotions of bereavement, and it can raise our spirits any day of the year by providing us with moments of playfulness, excitement, and astounding beauty.

Seven Common Questions About Lucid Dreaming

Despite the huge number of psychological and academic studies into lucid dreaming and a barrage of books, videos, articles, documentary films, and websites devoted to the topic, it seems there is still plenty of mystery around the practice of waking up inside a dream. I get asked the same questions again and again. They are excellent questions, so I'll briefly respond to a few of them here.

Can Anyone Have Lucid Dreams?

Yes—we all dream every night, and it's entirely possible for us to become aware that we are dreaming at any given moment. Many people experience spontaneous lucid dreams from childhood. It's very natural to become aware in our dreams.

Is Lucid Dreaming a Learnable Skill?

Yes—lucid dreaming can happen spontaneously, but we can also learn to become lucid in our dreams and increase the frequency of our lucid dreams by using the techniques and practices described in this book.

Should We Control Our Dreams?

When it comes to dream control, there is no should or shouldn't. Each person can work out for themselves how they'd like to interact with their dreams. One thing I've learned in my lifetime of lucid dreaming is that we are inseparable from our dreams; they are us, and we are them. So, it makes sense to engage respectfully with the people, animals, and worlds we encounter in our dreams. What some beginners don't know is that it's perfectly possible to be lucid in a dream and *not* guide the action, but just relax and go with the dream flow. However, it's also possible to guide dreams in endlessly creative, healing, and fun ways. The pros and cons of dream control are looked at in chapter 7 on how to guide lucid dreams.

Is Lucid Dreaming Dangerous?

No, it is not dangerous. Lucid dreaming can be wonderfully healing and beneficial in so many ways. However, for people who are highly emotionally fragile (for example, after a recent bereavement or other trauma), it's advisable to seek support from a professional therapist before diving into any deep introspective activity, whether it's meditation or lucid dreaming. This advice extends to people who are severely depressed or suffering from anxiety disorders or psychosis. When we work with our dreams—non-lucid or lucid—we come face to face with our deepest unconscious emotions and images, and it's good to be prepared for whatever we may encounter.

Can Lucid Dreaming Help Me with My Nightmares?

Yes—psychology studies show the usefulness of lucid dreaming for reducing nightmare frequency, and some psychotherapists use lucid dreaming therapy in their work with clients. Lucid dreaming gives us the ability to face a nightmare without feeling crippled by fear—when we realise we are being attacked by a *dream* hyena and not a real one, we can be brave and take steps within that nightmare scenario to make healing changes and gain insight into why we are having this particular nightmare. Chapter 8 explores the value of lucidity as a nightmare solution and offers ways of working constructively with nightmare material.

Is There Scientific Evidence of Lucid Dreaming?

Yes—a pioneering experiment was carried out by British psychologist Dr. Keith Hearne at the University of Hull on April 12, 1975. In the sleep laboratory, Hearne wired up a talented lucid dreamer, Alan Worsley, to an EEG machine to observe his brain waves and eye movements throughout a night of sleep. When Worsley became lucid in a dream, he remembered to carry out the pre-agreed signal: sweeping right-left eye movements that could be clearly seen on the EEG. This was the first deliberate communication between the dream and waking worlds, and provided the world with the first scientific proof of lucid dreaming. Since that date, there have been many repetitions of this experiment, and hundreds of research studies into lucid dreaming. *Llewellyn's Complete Book of Lucid Dreaming* covers the science, psychology, and history of lucid dreaming.

How Can I Get Lucid if I Can't Remember My Dreams?

How indeed! Non-lucid dreams are fascinating in themselves and they are also the gateway to lucid dreams. When we bestow them with love and attention, they blossom. The following practice gives tips on how to turn a dream recall drought into a welcome flood.

ᏮᏇ *Practice 1* ᏇᏮ
How to Improve Your Dream Recall

Remembering dreams is an act of awareness, and it's also an act of listening; a way of caring about ourselves and our rich inner life. It's wonderful to pay attention to this deep part of ourselves and notice the infinite ways in which dreams and waking experiences intertwine. Lucid dreaming is all about awareness. Improving dream recall can be viewed as a vital first step to securing that brightly shining awareness.

- Try not to use a stressful alarm clock, but wake up naturally, or to a favourite song.

- Using the same "wake up" song will condition you to recall your dreams while it plays.

- As you slowly wake up, don't move a muscle or open your eyes. Instead, think back and ask yourself, "What was I just doing? How was I feeling? Who was I with?" If all you recall is a colour or a mood or a shape, that's an excellent start. Write down anything you remember.

- Make a pact with your dreaming mind: send me some dreams I can actually remember, and I promise I'll write them down. You may find it helpful to write a letter to your dreaming mind, requesting excellent dream recall and greater lucidity. Sleep with the letter under your pillow.

- Whenever you wake up briefly in the night, automatically think back to what you were just dreaming about.

- Try taking afternoon naps because you'll go straight into a dream-rich sleep and are likely to recall dreams much more easily.

- The more often you remind yourself that you intend to recall your dreams, the stronger the message to your unconscious becomes, and your dreams will respond by coming to you.

When we remember our dreams, the next step is to make a note of them, as the following practice shows.

⟶ *Practice 2* ⟵
Power Up Your Dream Journal

If you're serious about lucid dreaming, it's valuable to keep a dream journal and get into the habit of noting down your dreams on a regular basis. This is to strengthen your connection with your dreaming mind. Dream images are alive. They have energy. It's fascinating to see what goes on in non-lucid dreams. It can be quite a revelation. The more intimately you know your own common dream themes, symbols, and stories, the easier it is to recognise when you are dreaming, and become lucid. It's possible to keep a powerful record of your dreams with minimal effort.

- It doesn't matter what you write on as long as you can read it afterwards. My own dream journals range from stunning hard-cover pocket notepads to the backs of crumpled till receipts. It simply doesn't matter, as long as you get the dream down. I have busy mornings because my child acts as my alarm clock, so sometimes I only have time to scribble down a dream while brushing my teeth or preparing food.

  My scraps of paper nestle in random places until I get around to transferring them onto my laptop or into one of my many dream journals. I've also been jotting down my daughter's dreams, and those notes tend to accumulate on the breakfast table. Okay, so it's not always a perfect system, but it works for us and those precious scraps always find their way into a more permanent record. The point is: no matter how hectic your morning routine is, you can always find a way to write down your dreams or speak them into a recording device.

- Sketch dream images, no matter your artistic ability! Images are so powerful and dream energy will come through even if they are rudimentary. Sketches help anchor you to the dream and recall it more easily.

- Keep your journal private so you can be frank and hide nothing.

- For each dream, write in the present tense to make the actions more immediate: "I'm floating along a dream cliff…" Create a title to remind you of the main actions and events.

- Use key words and jot down dominant emotions, then flesh out the details of the dream.

- Use a checklist of simple questions to ask yourself, such as: What's the story of this dream? What are my main emotions and actions? Is there anything I regret—what would I change about my reaction or the events in this dream if I could?

- Consider your associations with this dream—what do the people, animals, objects, or emotions in the dream remind you of? How about the colours and scenery? Often a current dream is connected with a current theme in our lives, and it can be insightful to grasp the connection. Some people like to leave a space under their dream account to add insights and make connections.

- Dream images are alive and their power shines through into our waking life if we allow it to, adding deeper meaning to our lives and illuminating our relationships and desires. Welcome them into your heart and be open to experiencing their aliveness.

- Return to your dream journal now and then to re-read your dreams. This will help you spot recurring themes or images, and you can use these as lucidity triggers by vowing to become lucid the next time you see that antique car again, or find yourself wandering the corridors of that spooky house.

As we become adept at recalling our dreams and inviting them into our lives, the next step is to work on building a lucid mindset, which can be thought of as the foundation for becoming a prolific lucid dreamer.

How to Create a Lucid Mindset

There are three golden tools that every lucid dreamer needs to cultivate in order to get and stay lucid, and successfully guide dreams. These are intent, clarity, and expectation (ICE). Intent is when we're determined to do something or make something happen; it's a powerful mixture of willpower and desire. Clarity means staying focused and clear-minded, even when we're being chased over a cliff by a dream serpent. Expectation is when we not only *hope* that something will happen, we *believe* it will and we are ready for it. When combined and reinforced, these three golden tools make up a lucid mindset.

We can practice these core lucidity tools while we're awake to strengthen them and increase our lucid dreaming frequency. We can also practice ICE while we're lucid dreaming to stabilise the dream so that it lasts much longer, to guide events, and to play around being lucid dream magicians by shape-shifting into animals or bestowing ourselves with X-ray vision or the ability to slow down time.

Developing intent, clarity, and expectation is really important for all aspects of lucid dreaming. It's a winning combo! To make sure you get a chance to strengthen these vital lucidity tools as you go through the book, I've structured it so the "get lucid" chapters include practices that focus on developing *intent*. The "staying lucid" chapters have practices that reinforce mental *clarity*, and the chapters on guiding dreams focus on working with the powerful tool of *expectation*.

If you work through this book doing the practices that appeal to you, you'll enhance your skills of intent, clarity, and expectation as you go along. You know yourself best, so you can spend as much or as little time as you need on these ICE-enforcing practices. Some people have a naturally high level of mental clarity and alertness, for example, and won't need to work on this aspect as much as others. This next practice is a great way for anybody to set their intent to have lucid dreams.

☜ *Practice 3* ☞
Create a Lucid Dream Goal to Fire Up Your Intent to Get Lucid

Why do you want to get lucid in your dreams? Here are just a few of the reasons I've heard from people who are trying to get lucid: "I want to experience night after night of dream sex." "I feel lucid dreaming will help me to advance spiritually." "I'd love to play at being God in the dream universe." "I need to heal psychologically/physically." "My goal is to experience non-gravity and the ability to fly." "I want to grab creative ideas from my unconscious!"

"I need help resolving my nightmares." "I want to develop my psychic abilities /intuition/empathy." "I want to explore the dream world like a virtual reality game." "I've heard you can meet deceased relatives in lucid dreams and I want to see my mother again."

Identifying the reason you want lucidity is helpful, because it helps you to create a highly specific lucid dream goal. This in turn helps you to cement the powerful intent to wake up in a dream.

- Write down your top three reasons for wanting to get lucid in your dreams.

- Pick a lucid dream goal by fantasising about the best, craziest, most beautiful, profound, or sexiest lucid dream you can imagine.

- Write down this fantasy lucid dream, then read it back to yourself, knowing that it *is* possible. Yippee!

- Harness this excitement and channel it into the firm intention to get lucid in your dreams.

- Every so often, return to your lucid dream goal to refine it or add new goals. This keeps you motivated, so it's good to always have a goal that really resonates with you, gets you wired up with curiosity, and ignites your desire to really go for this! Willpower and enthusiasm are key for kick-starting lucid dreaming.

- Although it's motivating and useful to have specific goals in order to keep your enthusiasm high, it's good not to become too fixated on achieving your lucid dream goals as soon as you get lucid in a dream. This is because it can be stressful to put so much pressure on yourself, causing you to wake up too soon. It may also crush the spontaneity and wonder that make lucid dreaming such an unforgettable experience. So, use your "ideal lucid dream" scenarios to get you lucid, and then once you're in a stable lucid dream state, be ready to either embrace or release your goal if it feels right.

The Stages of Sleep

The Art of Lucid Dreaming explores how important it is to be aware of the kind of sleeper and dreamer we are. Sleep is not separate from lucid dreaming—

it's the basis for it; the enabling factor. Chapter 4 helps you to look in depth at who you are as a highly individual sleeper and dreamer so that you can fast-track yourself to the best lucidity induction techniques for you. For now, let's take a quick look at the four stages of sleep that we pass through every night in a series of recurring cycles that take around ninety minutes each.

Stage One

This is the lightest stage of sleep; an easily interrupted, drowsy state with alpha brain waves in which our eyes roll slowly and we may experience sensations of falling or suddenly jerk awake.

Stage Two

This is a slightly deeper stage of sleep, the first non-REM stage (NREM) in which we are harder to rouse. Our brain waves slow overall to a theta rhythm, but with specific bursts of activity.

Stage Three

This is deep, restorative non-REM sleep, with slow delta brainwaves. It's hard to wake someone up from this stage. Sleepwalking, sleep terrors, and other sleep disturbances can occur.

Stage Four

This is where you will experience rapid eye movement or REM sleep. The body goes into muscular paralysis to stop us from acting out our dreams, but paradoxically, everything else activates: there is genital arousal, increased heart rate, eye movements (hence the name), and the brain waves are highly active and very similar to those observed during the waking state. REM sleep is associated with vivid and often bizarre dreams.

As we rotate through these four stages of sleep several times over the course of a night, the deeper sleep stages grow shorter, while the REM cycles grow longer. It seems likely that many lucid dreams take place during REM sleep, although not all do, despite what many people assume: lucid dreaming has also been detected in non-REM sleep stages.[4] Typically, we'll have the

---

4. Stumbrys and Erlacher, "Lucid Dreaming during NREM Sleep."

longest burst of dream-rich REM sleep at the very end of our night of sleep, around ninety minutes or so before we wake up. During this sweet spot, our brain chemistry is beautifully set up for lucid dreaming. Here's a practice to help you to capitalise on this optimal time for lucidity.

⟲∞ *Practice 4* ∞⟳
Early Morning Meditation to
Incubate a Lucid Dream

Meditation is excellent for lucidity training at any time of day, but falling asleep straight afterwards will increase your chances of getting lucid.

- Get up around two hours earlier than usual (I know—this is the hard part). But as we've just seen, there's a good reason for it: the final, long burst of REM sleep will happen as soon as you fall back to sleep, bringing rich and weird dreams to snap you into lucidity.

- Sit up in bed or at the end of your bed, and meditate. If you go all floppy or try to scramble back under the covers, be ruthless—force yourself out of bed and meditate on the floor with a blanket around your shoulders. Console yourself with the thought that you'll be back in bed soon enough, hopefully having an amazing lucid dream!

- Close your eyes and begin to meditate. Breathe slowly and evenly, allowing your thoughts to pass by without latching on to them. This can take some practice, so be patient with yourself if you haven't tried meditation before. It can help to focus on a ball of golden light in your mind's eye, or repeat a mantra to go with your breath, such as: "I breathe in light, I breathe out light." Change the colour of the light if you like, so that you are breathing in colour. Visualise the light illuminating your body with its warmth.

- Once you feel rooted in your meditation, as you continue to breathe peacefully, focus on an image of yourself, gloriously lucid inside a dream. Feel your mind and body fill up with lucidity: feel the clarity, the powerful happiness. Imprint on your mind and body this awesome feeling of being lucid in a dream. When you're really feeling this, set the firm intention to become lucid in your next dream.

- Summon a feeling of gratitude, as if your wish has already been granted. As you emerge gently from meditation, remind yourself that you have the natural ability to be conscious in your dreams. Smile, and as you settle back into bed, keep this lucid smile and the sense of calm contentment.

- Go back to sleep mentally repeating the lucidity mantra of your choice. Keep it simple: "I am lucid right now, lucid right now…" Be alert to imagery, strange sensations of falling or flying, and odd noises—this is the transitional stage from waking to sleep and you need to stay aware. If you succeed, you'll move directly into a lucid dream.

Sometimes we can follow all the recommended steps to becoming lucid in a dream and yet somehow, something invisible keeps tripping us up, and we don't manage it. This can be really frustrating! Before we jump further into the many practices in this book, let's first take a moment to explore the kinds of inner doubts or blocks that commonly prevent people from waking up in their dreams.

How to Dissolve Doubts, Fears, and Mental Blocks that Stop Us from Getting Lucid

If we harbour some dark or frightening belief about lucid dreaming, or simply believe it can't be done, our trip into the wonders of lucid dreaming has effectively been cancelled before it can begin. It's good to do a bit of soul-searching before we begin to try to get lucid to see if there is any unhelpful belief we're holding on to that might hinder our progress. Sometimes we don't even realise we have a resistance to lucid dreaming until someone else speaks up about their own doubts, so I hope it's useful for you to hear some of the arguments and fears people have shared with me, and how I commonly respond.

"It's impossible"

"I'm not convinced it's really possible to wake up in a dream. It's never happened for me!"

If there's an internal barrier telling you that you're shooting for the impossible, lucidity seems highly unlikely. Doubt is made from powerful stuff. Lucid dreaming is a scientifically proved aspect of normal sleep that appears in world literature stretching back centuries. If part of you doubts that waking up in a dream is possible, you could work on destroying that doubt by filling your mind with the scientific facts and historical and cultural reports.

We adults love to cling to our preconceptions. It's a breath of fresh air to explain lucid dreaming to a child and watch their faces light up as they get it—and in some cases, the very next morning, they'll bounce up to tell you they did it, they got lucid in their dream and faced that roaring bear that was messing with them! Adults can learn a lot from children. Train your mind to *fully expect* that you will become lucid in your dreams. We all dream every night, and we are all conscious during the day. To dream lucidly, we simply need to combine these two natural abilities.

"What stuff might come up?"

*"I had a tough start to life and I'm worried that lucid dreaming might
cause certain things from my past to come up that I don't want to face."*
Any introspective activity such as meditation or dreamwork brings us face to face with ourselves at the deepest level. Knowing this, it's for you to decide if you wish to pursue lucid dreaming. It's worth bearing in mind that lucid dreaming has enormous healing potential. I see this all the time in my personal dreamwork and in the workshops and retreats I lead, as well as in the large number of messages I receive from people who feel compelled to connect with me to share their experiences of facing past demons in lucid dreams, overcoming their worst nightmares, and meeting with wise dream guides in the form of powerful animals or dream people.

Sometimes it's helpful to ask ourselves why we are alive—are we here to survive, or to thrive? Personal growth can be painful and it can feel scary, but in the long term, the better we understand ourselves, the more we unlock our vast inner potential and the more we increase our ability to be kind and loving to others. For my part, I've found that the more I let dreams into my life, the happier and more balanced I become. After a lifelong close connection with my dreams, I view my dreaming mind as my best friend, because my dreams (lucid or otherwise) are always there to guide and help me through every difficulty in my life.

"It bores me"

"I'd love to get lucid, but the idea of doing reality
checks or keeping a dream journal bores me stiff!"

This is why I encourage people to invent their own reality checks and lucidity anchors. We are so different, and while some people will be fine using pre-prepared reality checks, others need something more creative and person-alised. As for dream journaling, it doesn't have to involve writing—you could draw your dreams, or record verbal dream reports. Being flexible and inventive is good. Make sure that nothing about the process of getting lucid bores you, because boredom is a real lucidity killer in any state of consciousness.

"I'm not creative"

"I'm not a creative or imaginative person.
They seem to find getting lucid so much easier."

Lucidity actually has a lot to do with logic—we need curiosity and logical thinking to cut through the stupor of not realising we are dreaming: "Elephants can't fly, ergo I am dreaming!" We need alertness, self-awareness, self-reflection, and critical thinking. We need a logical mindset to test the reality in which we find ourselves and discover it to be a dream. So the "I'm just not imaginative enough to get lucid" argument doesn't really work.

Besides, we are all inherently creative because we all dream. Look to your dreams and you'll soon begin to see how creative they (and therefore, you) are. In my work with creative writing and dreaming, I've met so many people who arrive at one of my workshops insisting that they are not imaginative or creative. But when they pick a dream or a nightmare and work from that, magic happens. They find themselves writing in a flow of original imagery, with rich descriptions and powerful insights. My Lucid Writing technique in chapter 6 shows how to do this. The point is, we can increase our imaginative reach when we tap into the super-creative source of our dreams. Once we release the idea of ourselves as being "not creative enough" to get lucid, we will have one less obstacle on our path to lucidity.

"I need rest"

"Lucidity sounds amazing and I really want it but I also just wanna sleeeeep! How can I get lucid without interrupting my precious downtime?"

This is what afternoon naps were invented for! Giving yourself a bonus rest will not only booster your resilience and creativity, it is the perfect time to get lucid: your body is tired, but your mind is relatively alert and your dreams will be vivid and strange, so it's easier to notice that this is a dream.

"It seems wrong"

"I'm intrigued by the idea of getting lucid, but dreams are sacred messages from our unconscious mind. Isn't it wrong to tamper with them by becoming lucid?"

This kind of preconception could understandably hinder a person's ability to get lucid—"wrong" is a very strong word and could result in a solid lock on our mind. Let's face it—if we believe it's fundamentally wrong to get lucid, we will likely find it very hard to start a lucid dreaming practice! Yet those who voice this concern generally aren't aware that lucidity and dream control do *not* have to go hand in hand. We can be lucid in a dream and not "tamper" with or change anything. Sometimes, the simple act of waking up inside a dream can spontaneously transform it in healing and spiritual ways. For this reason, lucidity itself could sometimes be thought of as the "sacred message" of the dream.

We love to put things into separate boxes, labelling them and rigidly dividing them. But how can anyone decide which state of consciousness is more sacred than the next? Consciousness is a flow that encompasses every single state, whether it's daydreaming, trance, dreamless sleep, non-lucid dreaming, lucid dreaming, or alert wakefulness. Each state is just as valuable as the next, because ultimately, they are all expressions of consciousness and human potential. Bringing lucid awareness to a non-lucid dream shines a light on our deep unconscious images and emotions, and this can be incredibly powerful. We can gain insight, self-understanding, and wisdom from becoming lucid in our dreams. Lucidity allows us to react spontaneously to dream events from a standpoint of greater awareness—just as we can when we work therapeutically with a dream while awake. In the highly responsive dream state, the potential for positive change is high.

Lucid dreaming is not reserved for levitating yogis and genius artists. Anyone has the potential to wake up inside a dream. We all dream every night, and we are all conscious during the day, so it's just a question of activating our conscious awareness *during a dream*. It's good to keep an open mind when trying to have lucid dreams and to question our habitual assumptions about dreams and reality. It can also be helpful to write down any obstacles we believe are stopping us from dreaming lucidly, then go down the list crossing each one out, knowing that it has no power over us. Mentally bathe these unnecessary obstacles in golden light and watch as they evaporate into thin air.

In lucid dreaming, one of the early lessons is about belief and expectation and how they marry us to particular outcomes. This works the same in waking life as it does in dreams! Sure, in a lucid dream, change can be instantaneous and profound, whereas in waking life things can be a little slower to manifest; but when we *expect and believe* that we are capable of becoming lucid in our dreams, we are planting a vital seed for the future.

———————

In this chapter we've looked at what lucid dreaming is and we've touched on some of the fantastic things we can do when we wake up in a dream. We've looked at the importance of intent, clarity, and expectation as golden tools for creating a lucid mindset, and how to overcome mental blocks to getting lucid. We've explored the value of setting a lucid dream goal to ignite our intent to get lucid. Hopefully we're all busily establishing a lively connection with our dreams by journaling and sketching them. Now let's dive into the most powerful practices for waking up inside our dreams.

CHAPTER 2

Powerful Practices to Help You Wake Up in Your Dreams

In our fast information age, more people are looking for "quick fix" lucidity. They might click on YouTube videos with beguiling click-bait titles like, "Get lucid in 30 seconds using this amazing technique!" But how can people who never recall dreams or who have a low level of waking lucidity hope to make the leap to dream lucidity in mere seconds? When we cultivate lucidity as a state of mind, using the vital forces of intent, clarity, and expectation, we can practise daily to raise our overall level of awareness, and this alertness finds its way into our dreams, too.

Sometimes people tell me they read online about a particular lucidity induction technique and tried it once, but it didn't work. This is like having one single driving lesson and then scratching our head in disbelief when we fail our test. It's helpful to stick with a technique for at least a few nights, and preferably a full week or more, to get ourselves used to it. The more we drum into our mind that we are doing this technique because we want to wake up in our dreams, the stronger our intention and expectation become, improving the chances of success. We also give our bodies a chance to adjust to techniques that involve waking ourselves up earlier than usual or meditating. Another good thing to do is tinker with the recipe by tailoring any technique to suit our personal style of sleeping and dreaming. We'll look at ways of doing that in this chapter.

Being motivated to get lucid is wonderful, but some people can get a little obsessed with the idea. Falling in love with an abstract concept isn't the best way to make it happen, and clinging too hard to the concept of "getting lucid" can stifle our creative engagement with lucid dreaming. People can end up feeling frustrated and disappointed every time they wake up without a lucid dream. They resort to techniques that destroy their sleep, such as setting the alarm clock every hour in an attempt to get lucid, and so end up exhausted! They berate themselves and feel unhappy about their progress. How demotivating is that?

It's far more helpful to be kind to yourself. Reward yourself for anything that feels like a step towards dream lucidity, such as recalling dreams, even the smallest scraps of dreams. Each remembered dream is a gift and can be seen as a step towards lucid dreaming. Perhaps one night in your dream you wonder, "Could this be a dream?" Even if you decided in the dream that you *weren't* dreaming, this is really encouraging as you were just one step away from getting lucid: give yourself a treat. Or you dream that someone is talking to you about dreaming—score! Your dreaming mind is helping you to get lucid. You dream you are flying—yes! Flying dreams commonly lead to lucidity.

Pat yourself on the back and smile when you spot any signs of increasing awareness in your dreams. Notice recurring dream people or objects and vow to pay close attention to them. Praise yourself when you manage it: "I'm taking vital steps towards lucidity—this is great news!" Thank anyone you can think of—the lucid dreaming gods or your great-auntie Nora who keeps showing up in your dreams and could be a fantastic lucidity trigger since she's been dead for twenty years. Gratitude is a powerful tool for manifestation. Hold the goal of lucid dreaming lightly and playfully in your mind as you practise the tools from this chapter, and keep your curiosity and motivation high.

Reality Checks

Dreams are bewitchingly real; they suck us into a three-dimensional, vivid, emotional reality with a strong story that we are totally caught up in. It can be hard to wrest ourselves away from the bewitchment and see clearly that this is a dream. Training our critical faculty enables us to successfully use logical thinking within the dream state. One way of doing this is to carry out reality checks as we go about our day.

Any time we pause to notice our state of consciousness and ask ourselves if we are dreaming or awake, we are doing a reality check: "Am I really awake right now? Could this be a dream? How do I know I'm *not* dreaming?" Whenever we take a moment to logically identify our current state of consciousness, we increase our chances of doing the same thing in a dream … and discovering that we are dreaming!

The reality check is an excellent way of increasing our ability to be fully aware in any given moment, whether we are awake or dreaming. It's a way of being mindful and focusing on this instant of our life. Doing this can help us live our lives in a more aware, alert way, and it can help us to get lucid in our dreams. The next practice explores the most effective reality checks to increase lucid dreaming frequency.

❦ *Practice 5* ❦
The Five Most Effective Reality Checks

Embed reality checks into your waking life and you'll find yourself spontaneously carrying out these checks while actually in a dream … and realising that you are in fact dreaming!

1. *The floatiness check:* a sense of floatiness in dreams almost always leads to lucidity for me; it is one of my absolute top favourite reality checks for that reason. Several times a day, tune in to the weight and solidity of your body. How light are you? Light enough to float? How substantial is your body? When you press your shoulder against a wall, do you begin to pass through it? If you slap a hand down on the tabletop, does it sink into the surface? Jump into the air—do you land with a bump, or hover a little? This is a fun reality test to perform,

although it may raise eyebrows if you try it during board meetings or on busy commutes.

2. *The finger test*: try to put your finger through the palm of your other hand. Really try for a moment. Expect it to work. Is your finger disappearing into your palm in a rather ghostly fashion? Has it popped through the other side? Then you are dreaming, my friend! This is a nice, unobtrusive reality check that can be practised almost anywhere and shouldn't get you kicked out of a meeting (as long as you only practise it on yourself). You can also pull the ends of your fingers to see if they stretch or even come right off. Stay cool if they do—they're clearly only dream fingers and will soon grow back.

3. *The nose pinch*: squeeze your nostrils closed, close your mouth, and breathe in. Is it difficult? Impossible? Do you feel like you're wearing nose clips in a pool? You must be awake. Do you find you can breathe just as easily with your nose and mouth tightly closed? Then you are dreaming.

4. *Telling the time or reading text*: if you wear a watch in your dreams or see a clock, observe it closely, because time is strange in dreams in more ways than one. The numbers on a digital watch may not appear in order, or become scrambled and the seconds won't be evenly spaced. Reading any text in a dream may be fine the first time you try it, but just try re-reading it! I have watched a perfectly stable sentence melt like ice cream in a dream, or spring confidently into a new, cryptic phrase. This is a fascinating way of exploring the creative energy of the dreaming mind, as it can generate the most surreal poetry you ever read (or create a pool of tasty ice cream).

5. *The hands trick*: this is a lucid dreaming classic. It has always worked for me. We usually have a dream body, so our hands are with us in our dreams, as they are in waking life. While awake—you can try this right now if you like—raise your hands to eye level, looking at your palms with curiosity. Observe the life lines and the gaps between your fingers, and now turn your hands over and look at the backs. Notice your rings if you wear any, examine those funny whorls of

skin on the finger joints, note the length of your nails. Look at the veins. Can you spot any freckles?

Familiarise yourself deeply with your waking life hands, and when you observe them in a dream, you'll notice tons of differences. People report seeing six fingers, fluffy palms, ghostlike translucent fingers, animal paws, melting digits, or simply someone else's hands! If your hands look fairly normal, try the "hand-flip": look at the palm of your hand, then flip it over to view the back. Then flip to look at your palm again, and so on. In a lucid dream, it's unlikely that your hand will look identical each time you flip it. Your fingers might appear in reverse order, or you might lose (or gain) a digit as you flip. I love looking at my hands in a dream because their appearance often comes as such a crazy surprise. And I get lucid right away.

There are lots of other reality checks, so take your pick, experiment, and you'll find one that works for you. For example, try closing one eye and looking at your nose. Can you see the curve of it? If not, you may be dreaming. Or try the tongue bite—see if it hurts when you bite your tongue. If it doesn't, you may be dreaming. Then there's the classic light switch test—in dreams, light switches often have a delay or don't work at all. Also, try thinking back to what you were just doing before this moment. Is there any logic to your movements? If you're at work right now, do you remember cycling there? If you're clinging to the spire of a cathedral, do you remember how you got up there? No? Well, then you've either had too many beers and accepted a silly dare, or you are dreaming.

Some people set an hourly beep on their digital watch by day and automatically ask themselves, "Am I dreaming?" whenever they hear the beep, but in my experience, this isn't the best idea, as it usually results in an automatic, half-hearted reality check. We are supposed to be training our critical faculty and our powers of observation, so a reality check should be prompted naturally. Doing reality checks on auto-pilot out of a sense of obligation is never going to get the best results. We need to find ways of creating spontaneous reality checks that are unique to us, using our body, our thought patterns, and our senses, as the following practice shows.

⁓ *Practice 6* ⁓
Invent Your Own Unique Reality Check

You are unique, so invent a reality check that reflects your uniqueness. When we link our senses, our bodies, and our habitual thoughts to a reality check, it grows in power and can be extremely effective.

- Have fun and be creative. One amusing example of a reality check came from a guy who told me that every time he farts, he asks himself if he is dreaming! There's no harm or shame in linking reality checks to the most intimate acts of our body—and no need to tell anyone how we anchor our intent if we prefer not to.

- If you're a smiley person, why not recall your intention to get lucid each time you smile at someone? If you often experience pulses of sexual arousal during the day, you could connect these to your desire to get lucid. Or if you have a singing gut, you could use stomach gurgles as a prompt to do a reality check. A knee that clicks? Use that click to help you develop a critical mind and question your reality!

- Notice when your body is *not* doing its usual thing. If you have any kind of chronic aches or pains, notice the spaces between the pains. In dreams, we are often pain free. We usually don't limp or hobble or have trouble rising from an armchair in a dream—we are able to race along without needing to catch our breath, or we jump like a gazelle. Notice, notice, notice … and you'll soon find yourself noticing when you are dreaming.

- Link certain thoughts to reality checks. If you are someone who regularly experiences negative or self-critical thoughts, you could react to this by using a reality check as a springboard into a lighter state of mind and imagine yourself flying over vibrant mountains in a lucid dream. This could have a happy double-whammy effect, both halting your negative thoughts *and* priming your mind to become lucid.

- Connect specific sensory sensations to reality checks. For example, every time you smell something amazing—freshly baked bread, your lover's perfume—ask yourself seriously: "Am I dreaming right now?"

- Change your anchor every so often so the challenge stays fresh and surprising. Whenever you see something that strikes you as particularly beautiful, ugly, or weird, ask yourself: "Am I dreaming?" Highly personal reality checks are likely to be the most effective ones for you. You'll find yourself so used to testing your reality that you'll soon find yourself doing it in a dream and realising that you *are* actually dreaming right now—how wonderful is that?

- Remember never to automatically assume you're awake. With each reality check, ask yourself, "*How* do I know I'm not dreaming this?" Look around, try to put your hand through the tabletop, or pinch your nose and try to breathe through it. *Expect* to discover that you are dreaming! This is vital, because you are training a critical state of mind that you will seriously need when you ask yourself "Am I dreaming?" in a dream. Only conclude that you are awake when you're 100 percent sure this is truly waking reality and not a dream. The rule of thumb is, if you're in doubt that you *might* be dreaming, then you generally *are* dreaming.

How We Can Use Our Memory to Help Us to Wake Up in Our Dreams

Have you ever thought something like: "I must remember to pick up some milk on the way home"? Yes, of course you have—we all make quick mental notes to do things in the future, and we act on these intentions all the time: we remember to get ourselves to that doctor's appointment and we remember to buy more windshield wiper fluid the next time we stop for fuel. This is known as prospective memory, and it is very much linked to intent. We *intend* to do something at a particular time, or on a particular occasion. The good news is that our natural ability to recall and act upon an intention can be easily linked to getting us lucid. We can do this in a number of ways. Try some of the techniques in this practice.

⟨⟩ *Practice 7* ⟨⟩
Use Your Memory to Get Lucid

This is a great way of strengthening your natural ability to remember to do things (stop by the store for orange juice; let the dog out; get lucid in my dreams).

- Remind yourself during the day: "Tonight, I am lucid in my dreams."

- Create reminder cues that stand out around your home or workplace and put them in spots where you will always see them. For example, you could write "Get lucid tonight!" on a sticky note and place it on the bathroom mirror so you see it while brushing your teeth. Carry in your pocket a small object that is linked in your mind to lucid dreaming, like a gemstone, or a tiny woven dreamcatcher.

- To vary things, set yourself a new creative task each day: "Today, every time I pick up a piece of paper or book, I'll say to myself: I am dreaming right now!" Or, if you're someone who travels a lot by car: "Today, each time I open the car door, I'll ask myself: Am I dreaming?" This is a great way of linking intent to reality checks and it creates continual reminders to get lucid.

- The point of all of this is that it *cements your intention to become lucid* by strengthening your natural ability to recall and act on things that you plan to do. Using your memory in this way will help you to remember during a dream that you intend to wake up inside that dream!

- Study your dream journal and pick out common objects, scenarios, or people who crop up regularly. You might notice you often dream of running to catch a train, or you may realise your mother is often present in your dreams. You might often see mirrors, clouds, or bananas in dreams. These are valuable lucidity triggers! Connect them to your intent to get lucid: "The next time I see fluffy white clouds, I'll know I'm dreaming."

This daytime practice can be expanded into the following practice to cement our intent by reacting differently to familiar stressors. It's helpful to personalise lucid dreaming induction practices so they suit our individual needs, and it's always good to experiment with ways of varying practices so they remain fresh and interesting.

ை *Practice 8* ை
Cement Your Intent by Day to Ignite It at Night

Every time we cement our intent to do something in particular *today*, and then do it, we reinforce our belief in the power of our own intent. But instead of taking the easy way out and choosing something we know we're bound to do anyway, like eat lunch or walk the dog, we need to bind our intent to something outside of our usual comfort zone, and see it through.

- Cement your intent to react in a new and different way to a familiar stressor; for example, decide you will bestow a big smile on your obnoxious neighbour, or resolve that you *will* be zen-like and patient when waiting in the next mile-long supermarket queue. A quick note here—there's no point in using your intent to deprive yourself of something you love, like chocolate, as this will not help you to get lucid (take it from me as a chocolate lover and high-frequency lucid dreamer). Bind your intent to doing something *positive*.

- In the morning, remind yourself as often as possible of your chosen intention.

- Devote a minute every now and then to visualising yourself carrying out your intended action. See yourself smiling radiantly at your grumpy neighbour, notice the astonishment on his face ... or do you spy the grudging beginnings of a smile in return? How does this strongly imagined interaction make you feel? Pay attention as the scene unfolds in your mind's eye.

- Make sure you carry out your intended action that same day (even if it means pressing your grinning face up against the neighbour's living room window—actually, no, I'd advise against doing that).

- Linking intent to an action that lies outside of our habitual range of emotions or reactions is not only a good practice for cementing intent, it is great for making us more open-minded and flexible towards life. An open mind is an excellent attribute for all lucid dreamers to cultivate, as it opens us up to the magical potential of this state of consciousness and enables us to take surprising dream events in our stride. This comes in handy as we venture more deeply into the world of lucid dreaming.

- Vary your assignment to keep you on your toes and make sure you don't get bored. You're allowed to be impish, creative, and childish. This is a game. Your intention one day might be to dance as if no one is watching you (perhaps close the curtains first so that no one is?), try out a repertoire of zoo animal noises (under cover of the stereo to avoid any escaped lion calls by concerned neighbours?), or you may choose to act out all of the parts in one of your favourite dreams.

- Regularly link your intent to waking up in your dreams. Create a mantra: "Tonight, I am lucid in my dreams." Believe it. Trust in your ability to make this happen. Remind yourself of your success with waking-life intent (shame about that restraining order from the neighbour though!) and feel certain that your intent is powerful enough to get you lucid in a dream.

Both of these daytime practices work well together with the following early-morning practice, which also relies on us remembering to carry out a future action.

⊙∾ *Practice 9* ∾⊙
The MILD Technique

The Mnemonic Induction of Lucid Dreams (MILD)[5] is a well-known technique that focuses on the ability to recall a pre-set task. It was developed by lucid dream researcher Dr. Stephen LaBerge, and it's nice for those mornings when you have the luxury of a lie-in. Here are the steps.

1. In the early morning, when you awaken from a dream, memorise it.

2. As you return to sleep, say to yourself: "Next time I'm dreaming, I want to remember to recognise I'm dreaming."

---

5. LaBerge, *Lucid Dreaming*, 155–6.

3. Visualise yourself back in that dream, only this time picture yourself becoming lucid in it.

4. Repeat steps two and three until your intention is clearly fixed or until you fall asleep.

Now we've looked at ways of using our memory to help us wake up in our dreams, we'll have a quick look at external lucidity triggers such as lucid dreaming masks and audio cues that stimulate us with light or sound while we dream, in the hope of penetrating our sleep with a strong reminder that *we are dreaming right now!*

Supplements, Lucid Dreaming Masks, and Audio Cues to Trigger Lucid Dreaming

In recent years, plenty of attention has been given to herbal supplements, amino acids such as choline, and over-the-counter drugs said to be helpful for inducing lucid dreaming. The Alzheimer's drug galantamine has been earmarked as a substance that lengthens dreaming sleep and promotes vivid dreaming. Studies show that it can also act as a lucidity enhancer, increasing the chances of becoming lucid in a dream.[6] Galantamine has side effects such as nausea and it is not compatible with certain medications. It can also worsen medical issues, including asthma, epilepsy, heart conditions, liver problems, and more. It's essential to check with your doctor before taking any supplement or drug.

My own take on supplements is that it's up to the individual to choose their own path to lucidity. In a lifetime of lucid dreaming, I've never taken any lucid dreaming supplements. This isn't because I have anything particular against the idea, but because I've developed my own deep, prolific, and highly effective lucid dreaming practice by focusing on waking up in all aspects of my life and using natural methods such as the ones in this book to trigger heightened awareness in my dreams. If you decide to try supplements or any mind-altering substances, ask your doctor about this first, and research any physical and psychological side effects so that you can go into it well informed and with a healthy respect.

---

6. LaBerge and LaMarca, "Galantamine Increases Likelihood of Lucid Dreaming."

Some people find lucid dream masks useful for triggering lucid dreaming. These take the form of an eye mask to wear during sleep. There are various models, some clunkier than others. Some rely on flashing lights that are intended to trigger lucidity, but these lights might flash as you're drifting off to sleep and wake you up since the mask can't recognise the onset of REM sleep. Often, people report they find the masks irritating because they either result in a sleepless night with no lucid dreams, or else the dreamer sleeps through undisturbed, not even registering the lucidity cues. As the technology gradually improves, an effective, comfortable lucid dreaming mask that results in high incidences of lucidity should arrive on the market. It just hasn't happened yet.

Even the best mask can't do all the work for us—we still need to plant the seed of intent in our mind and use our memory to connect it to the mask: "When I see flashing lights, I'll know I'm dreaming!" People report seamlessly incorporating the lights from lucid dreaming masks into their dreams—they dream of ambulances, discos, or UFOs—but if they don't manage to recall what those flashing lights really mean, they don't become lucid.

Another external lucidity cue that may work better for some are smartphone apps that use audio cues to penetrate the dream state. You could record your voice saying, "This is a dream—I'm lucid in my dream!" and time it to go off around five hours into your night of sleep. Sometimes these little tricks and prompts can become wonderful lucidity triggers; we just need to be patient and experiment to find what works best for us.

Nighttime Practices for Getting Lucid

Now we'll look at a range of nighttime lucid dreaming induction techniques. This next one is excellent for lucid dream induction. The Wake Up, Back to Bed technique (WBTB) uses brain chemistry in our favour. When people are deprived of REM sleep and then allowed to return to sleep, they then spend more time in REM to catch up. This is known as the REM rebound. The Wake Up, Back to Bed technique briefly interrupts our sleep in the early hours of the morning, enabling us to focus on lucid dreaming once we're past the deep sleep stage and our brain is active, geared up for a final, long burst of dream-rich REM sleep. Try it for yourself!

ꙮ *Practice 10* ꙮ
Wake Up, Back to Bed (WBTB)

It may take a bit of adjustment to work out the perfect time for you to do WBTB, but this is such a powerful technique that it's worth the effort.

- Set your alarm clock around five hours into your night of sleep. If you are someone who sleeps for less than six hours total, set the alarm four hours in to begin with, but you may need to adjust as you experiment with this technique. You don't want to end up wide awake for the final hours of the night. This is detrimental and won't get you any closer to your goal of lucid dreaming! Be ready to experiment to find a time that is optimal for you where you can easily fall back to sleep.

- Get out of bed when you hear your alarm clock to wake up completely.

- Write down any dreams you remember. For about twenty minutes, carry out some other dream-related activity, such as reading a lucid dreaming book or watching a YouTube video on lucid dreaming. Depending on whether you're a light or heavy sleeper, you may need to adjust the length of time you stay awake. If you're a very light sleeper, you may not even need to get out of bed for WBTB to be effective—just scribble down your dreams and return to sleep as per the final steps of this practice. Some heavy sleepers who find it hard to wake up and think clearly in the middle of the night may need forty-five minutes of wakefulness before returning to bed. Tailor this technique to suit you.

- Go back to bed. Relax deeply. Replay one of your dreams in vivid mental detail. Notice any strange images or events that could have been great lucidity triggers. Imagine becoming lucid in this dream and play out what happens next.

- Set a firm intention to become lucid in your next dream. Really expect and believe it will happen—get excited about it!

- Return to sleep repeating a mantra such as: "The next thing I see or touch is a dream" or: "I am dreaming now, dreaming now, dreaming now …" If your mind starts whirring away on a different topic, steer it firmly back to your lucid intention. Look out for pre-sleep imagery and keep one part of your mind alert as your body relaxes into sleep. You'll notice images beginning to form and move and flow into whole scenes … you are lucid in a brand-new dream!

You've probably noticed by now that I set great store on creative routes into lucid dreaming, ones that involve working with your uniqueness: your unique body, your unique mind. The more closely we tailor lucidity-induction techniques to suit the kind of person, dreamer, and sleeper we are, the faster we'll get lucid. First, let's look at ways of developing our own personal lucidity triggers and then move on to explore a range of further practices for waking up in our dreams.

໑๑ *Practice 11* ๑๑໑
Create Your Own Personal Lucidity Trigger

This practice gets you thinking about how your body and your dream content can help you to get lucid.

- Are you someone who dreams about needing the bathroom if you drink too many fluids before you go to sleep? Many people do—hunting for the bathroom is a common dream, and when we wake up with a full bladder, we understand in hindsight why we had that dream. But surely it would be better to realise *during* the bathroom dream … and become lucid? We can help this happen by purposefully drinking a big glass of water before we go to sleep, and reminding ourselves as we drift off: "the next time I need the bathroom, I will realise I'm dreaming!"

- This trigger can be adapted to suit whatever works best for you. For example, it might be effective for you to go to bed hungry one night, declaring with solid intent: "the next time I see food, I'll become lucid." At some point in the night, you'll find yourself gorging on dream pies or attending a dream banquet. Ding! You're lucid. You might try abstaining from sex for a few days to induce an erotic dream, and use that as a lucidity trigger instead. Experiment and see what works best for you.

- Identify your unique dream themes and symbols. Prime your brain to recognise these typical dream signs. Bring them into your falling asleep mantra: "Next time I'm fire-fighting/singing Sinatra songs /hanging out with my deceased grandmother, I'll realise I'm dreaming."

⟲∞ *Practice 12* ∞⟳
The Finger-Induced Lucid
Dream Technique (FILD)

Carry out this technique when you're really tired, perhaps in the middle of the night or as an extra boost when practising the Wake Up, Back to Bed technique from Practice 10. Lie still with your eyes closed, ready to sleep. Wiggle your forefinger and middle finger very slightly, as if you're playing two notes on a piano. Keep the rest of your body deeply calm and still. Gradually reduce this repetitive finger movement until it is a mere muscle twitch, but keep your full attention fixed on this tiny movement. Your brain is alert and active. It is sending a signal to your fingers to move, and they are responding, but ever so slightly.

Stay focused on this almost-movement as you fall asleep, combining it with a sleepy mantra: "I am dreaming, I am dreaming…" Then do a reality check—push your fingers through the palm of your other hand, try to float, or pinch your nostrils closed and try to breathe through them. *Are* you dreaming?

⟲∞ *Practice 13* ∞⟳
Compile a Lucidity Playlist

Gather some of your favourite songs on a playlist—but only choose a few songs, say three or four maximum. Then spend time turning each of them into a lucidity trigger by singing along to them, "I am lucid, this is a dream!" or by fiercely concentrating on doing reality checks the moment you hear them. There are apps that can be set to start playing music when you estimate you'll be in REM sleep (around four and a half to five hours into your night of sleep is often a good time), so connect your lucidity playlist to this, or set a timer on your phone to begin playing your lucidity-triggering songs at the allotted time. This triggers the trained response that you have carefully set up so that when you hear those lucidity tracks, you automatically ask yourself if you are dreaming.

The idea is that when your lucidity playlist seeps into your dreams, you'll *realise* that you're dreaming. This technique may require a few adjustments —the volume must be loud enough for you to register it in your sleep, but not loud enough to wake you up, and you may need to play around with the timing, too. Aim for the long period of REM sleep towards the morning, as this is a time where the brain is highly active and the dreams are weird and vivid, which makes getting lucid a whole lot easier.

⟨∞ *Practice 14* ∞⟩
The Stuck Arm Technique

This is simple but can work really nicely. Snuggle into bed and get cosy, but make sure that one of your arms is trapped (comfortably) under your belly. Then say firmly to yourself: "The next time I move this arm, I'll be dreaming!" Now visualise yourself swinging that arm around, pointing at something, or picking up an object, and imagine this action leading to the sudden understanding that you must be dreaming. Put all your awareness into that trapped arm as you drift off to sleep, and keep mentally reaching out with it and seeing yourself becoming lucid. Keep imagining this … and before you know it, it will actually happen; you'll shake hands with a kangaroo and realise with a jolt of happiness that this is a dream!

⟨∞ *Practice 15* ∞⟩
Use Mini-Awakenings to Cement Your Intent to Get Lucid

Make sure the very last thought you have before you drop off to sleep is about lucid dreaming. Not just when you fall asleep at the start of the night, but any time you wake up and then return to sleep during the night. We all wake up for brief moments many times in the night. These are often the moments when we shift position or turn over in bed. If you can raise your alertness enough to recognise some of these mini-awakenings, and quickly pull into your mind an intention to get lucid, you'll double your chances of having a lucid dream. This is because lucidity is more likely in the later stages of the night, when we are in lighter sleep stages and have longer phases of vivid dreaming.

If you're a fairly heavy sleeper, try turning onto your back when you experience a mini-awakening and saying mentally: "I'm lucid, I'm lucid" as you drift back to sleep. Anchoring your lucid intent to a particular sleep position turns this into a super-simple but effective lucidity ritual.

———————

In this chapter, we've looked at eleven core techniques to help you build your intent, sharpen your logical thinking about which state of reality you're in, use your memory and your body to help you get lucid, develop a relationship with your individual dream imagery, and fine-tune different practices to help you to recognise that you are dreaming *right now*. In the next chapter, we'll explore a vital gateway to lucid dreaming—the pre-sleep state—and I'll share my best practices for utilising this state and cultivating deep, alert relaxation to get lucid.

Chapter 3

Relax Your Way into Lucid Dreaming

When it comes to lucid dreaming, we can't relentlessly push and force ourselves and expect fabulous results. After all, we're talking about doing a remarkably subtle yet powerful thing: raising our awareness while we sleep. This is not the same as training for a marathon or cramming for an exam. When we try too hard to get lucid at the expense of a good night's sleep, we risk creating a new problem for ourselves—insomnia! It's vital to sleep well and dream well in order to take care of our body and mind. This means we need to master the art of relaxing deeply *and* remaining alert. Luckily, there are some great ways of learning this tightrope act. This chapter presents more core techniques for getting lucid. These focus on the entry point of sleep, where if we remain alert, we get to see a slideshow of bizarre imagery and experience strange and fascinating sensations as we drop off to sleep. This is a powerful gateway to lucid dreaming.

As you follow the practices in this chapter, you'll find they bring a multitude of benefits. They'll help you to become an adept lucid dreamer, someone who can easily balance alert mental attention with deep relaxation. They'll enable you to explore the marvellous creative world of pre-sleep imagery (known as hypnagogia). These practices will also bring you swiftly into a calm state of relaxed awareness, enabling you to let go of your worries and refresh your mind and body—a useful skill in any area of life. Techniques for deep relaxation and visualisation are excellent practices for beginner lucid dreamers as they teach us how to *relax* our way into lucid dreaming.

Let's take a guided journey into an intoxicating state of consciousness that we all pass through each and every time we fall asleep—only most of us fail to notice it because we lose consciousness immediately.

A Lucid Journey into Sleep

Every night, we lie down and relax, allowing thoughts and impressions of our day to skim through our mind, perhaps rewinding now and then to relive a particularly delicious moment—or to stress over something that went badly. As our body grows heavier, the bed warmer and cosier, we begin to release our hold on these thoughts. Our mind begins to drift. We are entering Stage One sleep, the lightest stage of sleep from which we can easily awaken. Have you ever been drifting blissfully off to sleep when a shocking jolt runs through your whole body and wakes you up? This is known as a "hypnic jerk" and it often happens as the body is transitioning from wake to sleep. Anyway, let's imagine in this scenario that there is no hypnic jerk, but instead something curious and rather delightful happens.

You can barely feel your body as you are so deeply relaxed, but instead of losing consciousness, you become aware that you are looking into a sort of luminous mist. Beyond the mist, you see distant, sparkling lights. You watch them sleepily, noticing how they move towards you and then away again. And now something surprising pops up in your field of vision—the face of a white wolf, startling in its detail and aliveness, but it remains only for a second before vanishing. Alert, you wait for more images. Here they come: something that looks like a bicycle innertube, swiftly followed by a flash of a complicated machine with whirring golden cogs, then a skateboard with muddy wheels…where are these random images coming from? You are caught in wonder, knowing that you are consciously experiencing the transition between waking and sleep.

And now the magic gets deeper. This parade of fleeting, two-dimensional, static images changes. The images remain in your visual field for two or three seconds, and better still, they become three-dimensional and begin to move. Here is a little girl in a purple dress, running across a garden. And now clouds are scudding through a twilit sky. You watch attentively, but you notice that when you try to follow the movement of a particular image, it dissolves. You quickly learn that you mustn't get attached. You cultivate a detached alertness, and this works better because now the images transform into moving scenes that play out like movies, short films that you follow as they self-create with astounding detail.

These films are bizarre (the surrealists knew what they were doing when they tapped into this state of consciousness). You sense they are flimsy in nature and could collapse at any moment and revert to the simpler, static imagery from before, so you don't get too involved in them, you simply observe. A whale soars through a stormy sky, white foam flecking the air. The reality of the imagery is incredible, like watching a colourful, richly emotional 3D movie. There's even a soundtrack: crashing waves mingled with an intense buzzing sound.

You realise you need to keep a clear head because this imagery is so beguiling and emotional. But you mustn't get sucked in. As soon as you think that, it's as if you're accelerating away from this scene; the whale shrinks to a tiny point above a vast ocean. The scene is all around you now—this is no longer like watching a film—you are *in* the film! You shoot backwards, lifting into space, and you think, "I'm an astronaut!" Instantly, you look down to see you are wearing a puffy white space suit and the earth is a blue and white marble far below. This is mad—your thoughts are influencing the imagery! Looking around, you see a million bright stars, and there are rolling green hills too, which is a weird thing to have in space. You alight on a hill with an oak tree and see the white wolf from earlier, only now it's standing a little way from you, its eyes as bright and alive as fire.

The closeness of the wolf gives you pause. Are you safe? Then you understand—you have succeeded in remaining conscious through the entire process of falling asleep! You have observed the morphing process of dream-building, and are now inside a full-blown dream—a lucid one, because you know for sure that you are dreaming! There's a curious aliveness to everything you see.

The detail is incredible. You can see every blade of grass, every acorn on the oak tree, and the gleaming eyes of the wolf, who you understand to be some kind of guide, a protective presence. Your lucid dream adventure has begun!

From Hypnagogic Imagery to Lucid Dreaming

Every time we fall asleep, we pass through the surreal, multi-sensory state of hypnagogia, a truly special portal into lucid dreaming. I established a six-stage model of visual hypnagogia[7] and the above account covers these typical stages: 1) formless mist, 2) initial light forms, 3) static 2D images, 4) morphing 3D imagery, 5) 3D film-like scenes, and 6) all-encompassing scenes. These stages can jump around, and what can happen when we're first getting used to this transitional state of consciousness is that we reach one of the later stages and find ourselves watching a dream film, but then it collapses back into the initial light forms, or we momentarily wake up thinking, "Damn—I lost it!" It's best not to be discouraged by this, as it happens to everyone. The steadier we can keep our mind, the greater the chances that we'll make it right through into a lucid dream.

Do you want to have this kind of experience? This is generally known as a wake-induced lucid dream (WILD) because we move directly from the waking state into the dream state with no loss of conscious awareness. On the journey into sleep, we not only get to experience strange hypnagogic images, but we may also experience a strange array of sounds and weird bodily sensations. We get to observe the transformation of static images into all-encompassing moving scenes and experience a new dream materialising around us.

Falling asleep while remaining consciously aware may sound like an impossible feat, but it is entirely possible and many people report success with this method. When you do it, it feels very natural. Once, I fell asleep consciously while watching a serene, life-sized image of myself lying on my back and floating headfirst into a glowing golden light. I remember watching this vision and saying to myself in wonder: "I'm falling asleep!" It was that easy: I simply watched.

Let's kick off with a practice so that you can try it for yourself.

---

7. Johnson, *Llewellyn's Complete Book of Lucid Dreaming*, 48–50.

⊙∽ *Practice 16* ∽⊙
Wake-Induced Lucid Dreaming (WILD)

This is an exciting way of entering a lucid dream, one that offers all sorts of surprises and bizarre sensations, so it's good to try it with an attitude of relaxed curiosity.

- It's easier to have a WILD either during an afternoon nap, or after around 4–5 hours of your night of sleep, when the deep sleep stages have passed and the brain is more active.

- Lie down and relax with closed eyes. Look into the darkness behind your closed eyelids and let your mind soar through this space. Don't get attached to the inner chatter in your head—let your thoughts pass by without engaging with them. If you find this part hard, use meditative music and deep steady breathing to help you to relax completely.

- Be receptive to whatever floats into your visual field. I often see a vibrant purple sphere as soon as I get into a relaxed, meditative state. Others see squiggles of light or grotesque faces emerging from the hypnagogic soup. Try to be cool about whatever comes up—don't allow yourself to be startled or fearful, as this will wake you right up and you'll be back to square one. Remind yourself that you are hovering on the threshold of dreaming sleep, and that you're bound to experience some odd visions and sensations as you traverse this threshold.

- Observe calmly as the imagery starts to move and change. Enjoy this private, surreal show. It can be delicious to float between the worlds of wake and sleep—and all in the name of "working hard" to become lucid in your dreams.

- As well as seeing a film-like flow of bizarre imagery, you may experience floating or falling sensations, loud buzzing noises, voices, the feeling that you are unable to move your limbs, or the sense of a presence in your bedroom. Don't worry—these are all normal events as your mind and body shift gears and the natural muscular paralysis that we all experience during sleep sets in. Chapter 8 explores sleep paralysis in more detail. All of these events and sensations can be welcomed because they are simply signs that you are in the process of falling asleep. Floating is great because you can simply *roll into a lucid dream* from here. As soon as you feel floaty or experience sensations such as falling or shooting upwards, this shows that you're already in your dream body. So simply picture a scene and roll your dream body right into it.

- If need be, remind yourself of this golden rule: if you become fearful, the imagery will become scarier. You are in an environment where your thoughts, emotions, expectations, and intentions shape what happens. You are a pure creative force! That's a good thing, but you'll need to stay calm and fearless. Try to keep an open, curious mind. Be scientific. Document the process. Take mental notes on what happens.

- Stay relentlessly alert. Do not lose consciousness—you're so close now! Stay aware and attentive. If this seems hard, repeat a lucidity mantra such as "I am *lucid* in my dream, *lucid* in my dream."

- At some point soon, the movie stream of imagery will leap into an immersive 3D scene with you in it, and bam! You'll be lucid dreaming.

- If this doesn't happen, create a scene in your mind's eye. This is usually easy to do in the hypnagogic state because imagery creation is what this state is all about. Picture a beach in the Seychelles and walk right into it. It can be that easy once you're so deeply relaxed that you don't feel your body. The imagery emerges bright and real: your toes sink into warm sand and the waves sparkle beckoningly … exotic holidays have never been so cheap!

- Sometimes you may end up floating in dark space, with no imagery and no dream body. Not to worry—you have simply found the lucid void. This is what I call "the gap between dreams" and you can rest here and enjoy this deep meditative space, or you can zip around exploring, or visualise a new dream and shoot into it. The void may seem uniformly black at first, but when you observe, you'll see colours and sparkles of light everywhere. This is the stuff that dreams are made from, so be prepared to watch a dream take form spontaneously right before your eyes as your lucid adventure continues.

Playing with the Lucid Dream Body

When I was a child, I used to spontaneously experience moments of physical expansion while awake, when I would suddenly feel much vaster than my little child's body. I thought of this experience as "Big Clare," and used to call to whoever was nearby, "Hey, it's happening again—look at me, I'm Big Clare!" They would glance at me, unimpressed, as I still looked the same size to them! I realised it was my inner perception that had changed, but it felt so real that it struck me as odd that I looked the same when it happened. Exciting, though. I looked forward to those episodes, which reminded me of the sensations I experienced in the dreams I thought of as "special." During that time of my life (aged between seven and eleven) I was journeying regularly out of my bedroom at night in lucid experiences where I would fly over the house and explore the garden and surrounding fields. I remember how utterly magical it felt to be in a body so light it could hover and fly; all I had to do was "think myself" in a particular direction.

Every night, we transition into a different body—our dream body. That body might look and feel more or less like our own (although happily it tends to lose all the usual aches and pains and is lighter and more flexible), or it might be the body of an animal we become in the dream. In some dreams, we are somebody else—we become our best friend or ourselves at a younger age. The dream body is a remarkable, flexible extension of consciousness. When we become lucid in our dreams, we can play with the dream body and do the most marvellous things. In waking life, we may be lying in a hospital bed, yet we can still dance with incredible energy and grace in our lucid dreams. In this way, we connect with the energy of a healthy, toned physical body and this can be a healing experience. The dream body is our ally and asset. Anything is possible.

I have performed delicious floaty backflips in mid-air in lucid dreams and turned myself into animals, birds, and objects, such as bouncy balls or stars. I have been male and female, old and young. I have used my dream body to fly, float, and dive through walls, mirrors, and doors. In my dream body, I can shoot up to the moon like an arrow or become multiple people simultaneously. I have purposefully made my dream body disappear atom by atom. We can choose to discard the dream body completely and become a floating point of conscious awareness, or dissolve into the dream air. When we mentally practise shapeshifting while awake but relaxed, we forge a trail to make this easier to achieve during a lucid dream. The following practice shows how.

⟋⟍ *Practice 17* ⟋⟍
Shapeshifting

I'd recommend this wonderfully creative practice not only for lucid dreaming induction, but for any time in your life when you experience a creative block. Shapeshifting teaches us mental flexibility and heightens our ability to get inspired.

- Lie down, close your eyes, and relax by taking a deep breath. Imagine all the tension flowing from your body when you exhale. Do this for several breaths until you feel your limbs grow heavy.

- In your mind's eye, play imaginatively with your body. Can you stretch as tall as the ceiling? Can you shrink down to the size of a hedgehog or expand to gigantic proportions? Can you inhabit the body you had as a child? How does it feel to be this size again?

- In your imagination, practice the arts of invisibility, weightlessness, and shapeshifting. Become the wind, or a cloud floating free, or an eagle soaring over an alien landscape. Become a raindrop that falls into a rushing river and flows into the ocean. Become a grain of sand, a lollipop, a sports car, or a race horse. There are no limits and you can have such fun with this (although on reflection, being a lollipop might not be so great—becoming an oak tree might be more relaxing than having someone bite your head off).

- Identify the moment you can't feel your body any more. Do this every night so that it becomes a habit. Recognise this as a sign that you are lucidly falling asleep, and remain mentally alert to what's going on— the weird imagery, sounds, and sensations of the hypnagogic state.

- Once you can no longer feel your body, create a scene in your mind's eye, one where you're doing what you would love to do in your ideal lucid dream. Feel your dream body—are you a person, an animal? What can you do in this body? Play with your ideas but stay focused and carry out the occasional reality check. Soon you might notice that you have in fact fallen asleep and that everything you see and experience is a dream.

The Pre-Sleep State as a Creativity Elixir

In states of deep relaxation where we are close to falling asleep (or waking up from sleep), the boundless creativity of dreaming mingles with our active, waking brain. This mixture is potent. Famously, the chemist August Kekulé discovered the correct structure of benzene while in the hypnagogic state. In *The Committee of Sleep*, Deirdre Barrett recounts his discovery. Struggling with his work on the possible structure of benzene, Kekulé gave up for a moment to doze in his chair. Alert to his pre-sleep imagery, he watched atoms twisting and turning in snake-like movements. He wrote: "But look! What was that? One of the snakes had seized hold of its own tail, and the form whirled mockingly before my eyes. As if by a flash of lightning I awoke…"[8] Kekulé then made a major breakthrough: he realised that the benzene molecule was not a straight chain, but a ring.

Inspirational ideas in art and literature have also been attributed to this in-between state of consciousness. Surrealist artist Salvador Dali used to nod off in an armchair holding a key which would drop as he fell asleep, making a noise that woke him up again. He did this to capture bizarre hypnagogic imagery as inspiration for his paintings. The good news is, you can access this creative state every time you fall asleep or wake up—and if you become lucid in a dream, you enjoy the same mix of dream creativity and an alert brain. You can ask how to solve a specific problem, or invite ideas for original artwork, and you may find that the response is astonishingly spot-on.

⁓ *Practice 18* ⁓
Surfing on the Edge of Sleep

Let's look at how to hover at the gateway of pre-sleep imagery without going through it unless we consciously choose to. It's an excellent lucidity practice to learn the art of staying mentally alert while our body floats on the cusp of sleep. This is also a powerful mindfulness practice. Hypnagogic imagery is by

---

8. Barrett, *The Committee of Sleep*, 86.

nature fickle and unstable, but at the same time it's so beguiling that it sucks us in. Staying aware and alert in the face of this combination is not easy. Let's face it, most of us don't even notice passing through this state of consciousness because we immediately release our conscious awareness and simply fall asleep!

When we play with mental imagery in a deeply relaxed state, we are surfing on the edge of sleep. What do we need to surf? Waves, a surfboard, and balance. In the hypnagogic state, waves are the streams of fickle imagery that disappear and reappear without warning. The surfboard is our stable lucid awareness. But no matter the quality of the board, we won't be able to surf unless we can stand up on our board and keep our balance. That takes practice, along with the understanding that we'll fall off our board plenty of times before we master the art of surfing. But no practice is wasted, so you can be pleased with yourself every time you try this exercise.

- Lie down somewhere not too comfortable, like a yoga mat (not in your bed).

- Adopt the "corpse pose" or *savasana*, a yoga pose where you lie on your back, legs outstretched and slightly apart, arms slightly away from your body, palms facing up. Close your eyes.

- Carry out a progressive relaxation: while breathing slowly and deeply, take your attention to your left foot and consciously relax it by flexing the toes and the sole and then releasing. Now take your awareness slowly through your entire body, tightening and then relaxing each body part as you go. Don't forget your jaw, eyes, and tongue. Feel your body sinking more deeply into the ground, and your breath falling into a natural rhythm.

- Pick a dream you had—one that speaks to you emotionally. Bring this dream vividly into your mind's eye and allow the imagery to move and change. Imagine you are lucid in this dream—what do you do next?

- After a time, you'll notice hypnagogic imagery emerging and your mind starting to drift. This is your signal to get more alert! Drifting means you're in Stage One sleep. Every time you feel yourself drifting off, pull yourself back and concentrate on the imagery again. Make sure you are in control. Keep yourself surfing close to the outer edges of sleep, but don't let the waves carry you right in. Bite your tongue lightly to bring you back, or even open your eyes just for a second if you are falling too deep.

- If you want to benefit from the creativity of this state, now is a good time to throw some thoughts about a current project into the mix, or daydream about an artwork you'd like to create. Stay easy and relaxed, don't force a thing. Open-ended questions that invite creative responses are good: "Which colours and shapes could I work with next?" Or: "What direction might my theatre project evolve in?" "How can I solve the communication problem with Angry Gavin from work?"

- Identify that precious moment when you can't feel your body any more. Stay lucid and alert, balancing lightly between states of consciousness. This is beautiful lucidity practice—well done for getting this far!

- After balancing between wakefulness and sleep for as long as you like, either return to wakefulness by wriggling your fingers and toes and taking a deep breath, or deliberately choose to surf right over the edge, into the heart of sleep—taking your full conscious awareness with you so that you surf straight into a lucid dream.

Transitions into the Waking State: False Awakenings and Hypnopompic Imagery

Although this chapter focuses on the entry point of sleep, I'd like to mention two experiences that happen as we transition from dreaming to waking up. The first is the incredibly disorienting event known as a false awakening. Have you ever had this? It happens when we wake up, get out of bed, brush our teeth, shower, get dressed … and then suddenly we wake up for real and discover that we're still lying in bed. Deeply confused, we realise we dreamed all those actions and now have to get up and go through them all again!

It's amazing how neatly the brain can trick us. Sometimes false awakenings can happen several times in a row so that we no longer know if we're waking or dreaming. This is actually a great opportunity to get lucid, so always do a reality check such as trying to hover off the ground, and remember that if you *suspect* this is a false awakening, then it very likely *is* one! This means you are dreaming and can lucidly explore.

The other experience that can happen as we wake up is hypnopompic imagery. This can seem identical to the pre-sleep hypnagogic state, but there are also many reports of imagery manifesting in the dreamer's bedroom and lingering there even after the dreamer feels fully awake, so that this state can seem closer to a waking vision than inner imagery. Again, it is a lucid state, so hold on to your awareness and observe the imagery or visions calmly, fearlessly, and with kindness in your heart. See chapter 8 for how to react to frightening imagery. If you view these sleep-exit states as further chances to get lucid and discover more about the weird and wonderful world of dreams, you'll be on the right track.

Core Skills to Increase Intent

Let's look at some other good ways of inviting lucid dreaming into our life by practising core skills to build our intent to get lucid, and by paying more attention to our physical body.

⟋⟋ *Practice 19* ⟋⟋
Sleep Under the Stars ... or at
Least in a Different Room

When we sleep elsewhere, we tend to sleep more lightly, with more frequent awakenings. The sounds and scents are different, the lighting is not what we're used to, the mattress is lumpier than our own, the duvet warmer. For heavy sleepers, spending a night on the sofa or pitching a tent in the garden could result in a greater likelihood of getting lucid, especially if we create a solid intent to wake up in our dreams that night. Alternatively, stay in your own bed but try going to sleep sitting up, or prop yourself up with extra pillows under your head or feet to prompt you into lucidity during the night. It could also be helpful to adjust the light levels in your bedroom so that it's a little brighter than what you're used to. Of course, any technique that disrupts your sleep should be practised with caution and not every night, because sleep is essential for our good health, so go easy on this one.

I know some people who have a "lucid dreaming nest" in their home that they sleep in when they plan to have a night of lucid dreaming. Undisturbed by your bed partner's snoring and free to put on the light to record middle-of-the-night dreams or practice the Wake Up, Back to Bed (WBTB) technique without anyone throwing pillows at you and yelling "just let me sleep!", this can be an effective practice for creating a rock-solid intent to getting lucid.

⌾⌾ *Practice 20* ⌾⌾
Become a Dedicated Daydreamer

This is a marvellous practice for lucid dreaming. There's no need to feel guilty when someone catches you gazing dreamily out the window—you can tell them you're engaging in important lucidity training. Yes, even if you're indulging in sexual fantasies or imagining test-driving a Ferrari. Daydreaming mingles fantasy with waking consciousness, and whenever we do it, we are taking one step closer to dreams. Just let your mind drift into a scenario and follow it through, sometimes rewinding the action and replaying things in a different direction. Become a movie director and guide events, bring in interesting characters, dialogue, colours and sensations—have a ball with this! You are the all-powerful creator of your daydreams. Link your faith in your daydreaming abilities to your intent to wake up in your dreams and have similar adventures while lucid dreaming.

⌾⌾ *Practice 21* ⌾⌾
Dream Reliving

This is creative daydreaming with a twist: instead of your usual daydreaming topics, take a previous dream as a starting point. In your mind's eye, relive your dream in startling detail: curl up with your dream tiger, go flying through the Milky Way, or visualise yourself having the best dream sex of your life. Change the dream as you like and imagine yourself lucidly navigating it. Dream reliving is excellent practice for lucid dreaming. For best results, ignore everyone else in the office and lie down and relax to make your dream reliving extra vivid. They can step over you on their way to the coffee machine! Seriously, though, deep relaxation techniques and powerful visualisations can work with an existing dream to send a strong message to your unconscious mind that your intention is to *wake up* in a dream.

⟡ *Practice 22* ⟡
Start a Bodywork Practice

Tai chi, yoga, expressive dance, or zen walking are just some of the many practices that increase body awareness. The more often we spend time bringing our awareness into our physical body and tapping into the flow of energy throughout our limbs, the more likely we are to notice when we find ourselves in our light, floaty dream body. This is one of the best lucidity cues because our body doesn't feel exactly the same in a dream as it does in waking life—not if we stop to check in with it. Train your body awareness and notice everything about how your body feels and looks, and how it interacts with the environment.

For example, does your hairstyle affect the way the waking world looks? If you have coppery spirals of hair bouncing around your face, as I do, these are your frame for viewing the world. Funnily enough, I've never once noticed my curls framing my vision in lucid dreams … this is another personalised reality check. Notice also your height and posture, the tightness of your jeans, the jiggle of your breasts, the weight of your feet on the ground. Are you ever aware of these things in your dreams? A simple reality check such as jumping in the air and seeing if you come back down to earth with a bump can be really helpful. And remember—if you are unsure enough about the reality in which you find yourself to feel the need to test it by jumping around like a frog, then it's pretty safe to assume that you are dreaming.

If moving around is difficult for you, or if you fancy a different approach, some lucid dreamers report that acupuncture triggers lucid dreaming. Brazilian novelist Krishna Monteiro first read about this in *Llewellyn's Complete Book of Lucid Dreaming* and tested it for himself. He had two acupuncture sessions in two weeks, and was excited to have lucid dreams following each session. Krishna told me that the acupuncturist worked mainly on the crown of the head and between the eyebrows, stimulating the crown chakra and the third eye chakra. If you aren't phobic about needles, it could be worth a try!

✄ *Practice 23* ✄
Hone Your Strangeness Radar

Notice beauty and strangeness as you go about your daily life. Is that a *duck* up in that tree? Oh, no—just a massive pigeon, but for a moment your eyes fooled you. Do a reality check. Wow, look at the snow nestling on top of those bright orange berries—how beautiful against the grey sky! Are you lucid dreaming? Someone has put a child's lost bobble hat on top of a large rock at the local playground, turning the rock into a weird gnome. Could this be a dream playground? Allow this ability to *notice* to creep into your dreams: out-of-place objects, an unusual person, an animal that speaks, a strange location, a bizarre or improbable event. All of these should prompt you to do a reality check. View all of life as a waking dream and ask yourself regularly, "Am I dreaming right now?"

✄ *Practice 24* ✄
Create a Lucidity Ritual

Being ritualistic about lucid dreaming can help to create the right intent so that our mind is geared up to realise we are dreaming. Some people find a serene, candlelit bath followed by ten minutes of meditation before bed, along with a lucidity trick, such as holding a lucid talisman in their hand all night, increases their chances of having a lucid dream. Consider a mix of the following elements when you create your lucidity ritual:

- A meditation practice such as the one in *Practice 4: Early Morning Meditation to Incubate a Lucid Dream*.

- A dream reliving exercise such as Practice 21, or set a visualisation to music along the lines of the next practice in this chapter: *Practice 25: Create a Pre-Sleep Visualisation to Trigger Lucidity*.

- It's good to finish off your lucidity ritual with the observation of pre-sleep imagery, as in *Practice 18: Surfing on the Edge of Sleep*.

- Combine these elements with a little "trick" such as writing down your intention to get lucid on a piece of paper and putting it under your pillow, or trying to hold a lucid talisman in your fist all night to remind you to get lucid.

Your talisman might be a sparkling crystal or a handwoven dream-catcher, but it could just as well be a ball of cotton wool or a paper-clip. As long as you imbue that paperclip with your intent to get lucid, it'll work just as well as any other object. It's all about intention and remembering to do reality checks whenever you become aware of your fist closed around your talisman.

Create any pre-sleep ritual you like, and carry it out on the nights when you are seriously chasing a lucid dream. Be sure to integrate your favourite practices for getting lucid into your chosen ritual.

⊙◦ *Practice 25* ◦⊙
Create a Pre-Sleep Visualisation to Trigger Lucidity

You can easily create your own effective, highly personal, pre-sleep visualisation to trigger lucidity. This is also a great way of reconnecting with dream energy before you go to sleep. It works best with a positive dream. However, you could also choose a dream that you'd like to change and imagine yourself lucidly guiding it to a more satisfying conclusion before writing down your new, recreated dream. There are many tips on doing this in chapter 8 on nightmares.

- Choose a vivid dream, one that left you with a strong impression.

- Sit with closed eyes and mentally re-enter your dream. Conjure it up in bright detail and feel the emotions you felt at the time.

- Imagine yourself becoming lucid in this dream and imaginatively play out what you do next.

- When you have been through the whole dream and feel thoroughly connected with your own dream energy and happy with how events play out, write down your visualisation. Use the first-person present tense ("I am dancing barefoot on a giant steel drum, creating deep sounds with my feet...") Insert as much detail as possible, and use your senses to bring the dream to life with scents, colours, sensations, emotions, tastes, and sounds.

- You are now the owner of a personalised lucid-dream-triggering visualisation. Keep it by your bed and whenever you want to get lucid, read it before turning out the light at bedtime. Alternatively, a good way to work with this visualisation is to record it on your phone, then get comfy in bed and listen to it. You can further customise it by adding a general relaxation at the start and repeating your chosen lucid dreaming mantra at the end. Just remember to speak slowly in a soporific tone of voice and leave plenty of pauses so there is time to create a vivid mental picture of the dream.

- Get cosy and relax. Allow your thoughts to settle. When you're ready, dive into your visualised dream. Luxuriate in it, knowing that connecting to your dream energy in this way will help you to get lucid in your dreams.

- Repeat a mantra to yourself as you fall asleep, such as: "Tonight I wake up in my dreams" or, "I am lucid, I am lucid ..."

- Change the dream in your visualisation script regularly for variation and to keep the exercise fresh.

A Lucid-Dream-Triggering Visualisation

Here's an example of a visualisation based on a powerful dream I had in 2018. You're welcome to borrow it if you like it, or get a friend to read it to you while you drop off to sleep.

> Your whole body feels deeply relaxed. Your mind grows calm and still. As you lie comfortably, feeling very calm and relaxed, you see a scene forming in your mind's eye, and you realise that this is your dream coming to you.
>
> You are standing happily on the strong stone balcony of a wonderful tropical hotel at the edge of the jungle. You have been watching the most magnificent orange and purple sunset, and now dusk is beginning to fall. The air is warm and crickets are singing. From your third-floor balcony, you can hear the refreshing splash of fountains in the hotel courtyard, and the exciting sounds of animals calling in the jungle.

Looking down towards the green jungle, you are astonished to see the animals emerging! Whole families of tigers and leopards with their babies and young gambolling and playing around them. There are giraffes and zebras. They all seem engaged in some kind of game or performance, frolicking around the hotel fountains to drink and play at the end of this hot day. The animals are having an amazing time and you see other hotel guests watching this spontaneous show from their balconies.

Then, out of the semi darkness, you see a huge tiger face looming right in front of you—how can this be possible? You're up on the third floor; it's impossible for a tiger to float suspended in midair, right? With a gasp of recognition, you understand that you are dreaming. This is a magnificent dream tiger, and it has come to visit you!

In awe, you look your dream tiger in the eye. Gracefully, it bounds onto your balcony. Its huge head is inches from your body, you can see each one of its whiskers and the glow of its wise amber eyes. You know it means you no harm. It's as if it wants to offer you its power, strength, and protection. It wants to be your friend. Laughing in delight, you find yourself floating up into the air. "I'm dreaming this!" you say in wonder. Your beautiful dream tiger levitates with you and you get the strong feeling that you have known each other forever; it's like meeting part of your own soul. Together you turn slow somersaults high above the jungle as the stars begin to come out one by one.

As you play in the sky with your tiger, you repeat to yourself over and over with perfect lucidity: "I am dreaming, this is a dream … I am dreaming, this is a dream …"

In this chapter, we have explored ten more powerful practices for getting lucid, focusing on the entry point of sleep. We've looked at the beguiling nature of pre-sleep hypnagogic imagery and how to successfully enter wake-induced lucid dreams (WILD). We've played with shapeshifting and explored the lucid dream body as a flexible extension of consciousness. We've looked at the creative possibilities of the pre-sleep state and seen how to surf on the very edge of sleep by playing with mental imagery in a deeply relaxed state. I've shared core skills to help you increase and solidify your intent to get lucid in a dream, and we've looked at how to create a highly personalised pre-sleep visualisation to trigger lucidity.

Now it's time to encounter one of the cornerstones of *The Art of Lucid Dreaming*. In the next chapter, you'll take the Lucidity Quiz and discover how to tailor-make your own Unique Lucidity Programme using the lucid dream induction techniques that fit you best as a unique sleeper and dreamer.

CHAPTER 4

Create Your Unique
Lucidity Programme

Now that we've looked at core techniques for getting lucid, we're going to get to know ourselves better as unique dreamers and sleepers. The keystone of this chapter is the Lucidity Quiz that I've created to help you identify the type of sleeper and dreamer you are. Based on your quiz results, I'll show you how to identify your best personal lucid dreaming techniques so you can custom-make your own powerful Unique Lucidity Programme and fast-track yourself to the lucid dream life of your choice.

What Kind of Dreamer and Sleeper Are You?

Sleeping and dreaming is universal: we all do it, every single night. But despite its universality, have you considered how *personal* sleeping and dreaming is? We all have different sleep habits: we sleep for different lengths of time, some have trouble dropping off to sleep, others sleep like logs. Some people tell me they never remember their dreams (a sad but treatable state of affairs), while others say their dreams come at them like machine gun fire as soon as they close their eyes and they ask me how they can get their dreams to calm down (pre-sleep meditation helps). There are "natural" lucid dreamers who get lucid effortlessly on a regular basis, and others who wish they could ramp up their lucid dreaming and spend more time consciously exploring their dream world.

In the spirit of honouring these and other differences, with an eye to encourage you to dig deeper into the whole sleeping and dreaming part of your life, I've invented the Lucidity Quiz. This quiz is based on the questions I ask people when I do one-to-one mentoring sessions. I like to get a clear idea of the kind of dreamer I'm working with so I can fast-track them towards the lucidity techniques that are most likely to work for them. We are all unique. The more aware we are of the type of sleeper and dreamer we are, the easier it is to handpick the best, most effective lucidity techniques for us.

❧ *Practice 26* ❧
The Lucidity Quiz

If you take it upon yourself to analyse the kind of dreamer you are, you'll bring deeper understanding to your entire sleep and dream experience. You'll also have a greater chance of success in becoming lucid. This quiz is a key feature of *The Art of Lucid Dreaming*. Your highly individual responses to the Lucidity Quiz will form the basis of your Unique Lucidity Programme: a customised set of lucid dream induction techniques to fast-track you towards lucid dreaming. A little further along in this chapter, I'll help you to create your own programme.

The best way to take the Lucidity Quiz is to set aside twenty minutes or so to sit quietly and write down your answers. If you're not keen on writing, you can speak your answers into a recording device. It can also be useful to get a friend to ask you the questions, because when we skim through a list of questions without really bothering to answer them fully, we miss out on a surprising amount of information. Whenever suggested answers are written in the quiz, these are only there to get you thinking, and there's no need to choose any of them—make your answers as individual and true as you can. The quiz is divided into sections to make it easier to navigate, as it's pretty in-depth.

Depth and Quality of Sleep

- How many hours a night do you sleep on average?
- How deeply do you sleep? (e.g., lightly; deeply; hard to rouse; feels like I barely sleep at all)
- Are you aware of waking up often during the night?
- Are you someone who loves snuggling in bed in the mornings, drifting in and out of sleep, and revisiting your dreams?
- Do you generally wake up feeling exhausted, energised, woozy, clearheaded, depressed, or joyful? Find the right words for you.
- On a scale of 1–10, how happy are you with your current sleep quality?

You and Your Dream Life

- How many dreams do you remember each morning?
- Do you make space in your life for your dreams? If not, why do you think this is?
- Do you feel that dreams have meaning? (e.g., symbolic, psychological, spiritual)
- Do you mainly have happy dreams, anxious dreams, dreams of being chased or attacked, or hurly-burly action-packed dreams? "Mundane"-seeming dreams, like queuing in the supermarket? Quiet dreams of calm and light? Find the words that best describe your dream content.
- Do you think something that happens in a dream can affect your waking life in any way? (e.g., mood, physical body, emotional reactions, life events)
- On a scale of 1–10, how happy are you with your current dream life?

Childhood Dreams

- Can you still recall particular childhood dreams and nightmares?
- Did you grow up in a family supportive of dreams? Think back to how your parents or teachers responded when you shared dreams or nightmares as a child.

- Did you have any memorable consciousness-related experiences as a kid, such as leaving your body, lucid dreaming, sharing the same dream as another person, or dreaming a future event that came true?

Imagination and Visual Thinking

- Would you consider your imagination to be: a) wild, free, and unstoppable, b) vivid and inventive, c) average d) you don't consider yourself an imaginative person.
- If someone leads you through a guided meditation or imaginative journey, is it easy for you to follow this and does your mind produce accompanying visuals, or is it more like just listening and not seeing anything?
- What kind of waking daydreams and fantasies do you indulge in, if any?
- Are your daydreams similar to the kinds of dreams you have at night?
- If you close your eyes right now and visualise an apple, how clearly do you see it?
- Would you describe yourself as artistic?

Nightmares

- Do you have nightmares? a) never, b) only as a child, never now, c) rarely, d) at least six times a year, e) monthly, f) weekly, g) nightly!
- How high is the anxiety level in your nightmares? a) relatively low, b) high, c) unbearable, d) I'm scared to go to sleep because my nightmares are so terrifying.
- Do you have scary pre-sleep imagery or frightening lucid experiences where you feel consciously aware but unable to wake yourself up?

Insomnia and Sleep Disturbances

- Do you suffer from insomnia (defined as lengthy periods of sleeplessness or an inability to fall asleep)?
- Do you sleepwalk, sleep talk, act out your dreams, experience sleep terrors (where you scream and thrash and generally don't recall anything afterwards), or experience sleep paralysis (where you feel locked in your body and unable to wake up)?

- If you experience periods of sleeplessness during the night, do you find this irritating and debilitating, or do you welcome this as time for creative thinking and fantasy?
- Do you often feel sleepy during the day?

Depression and Anxiety

- Have you ever experienced periods of anxiety or depression?
- Do you ever cry or feel depressed and worried in your dreams, or wake up suddenly in the night feeling anxious?
- Are you currently taking medication for anxiety or depression? (Medications can have a strong effect on dreams, repressing or activating them.)

Awareness

- What is your most usual level of awareness in your dreams? a) regular lucid dreams with stable lucidity, b) occasional lucid dreams, some difficulty staying lucid for long, c) fairly aware but not fully lucid, d) non-lucid, e) deeply non-lucid.
- How conscious are you in your waking life?
- How often do you feel fully, gloriously alive?
- Do you examine your state of consciousness while awake? And in your dreams?
- In non-lucid dreams we assume we're awake until we wake up for real and realise we were dreaming. How do you know you're *not* dreaming right now?

Lucid Dreaming

- Do you have spontaneous lucid dreams?
- Do you think lucid dreaming is easy, hard, dangerous, transformative? Find your own words.
- How often have you experienced lucid dreams?
- Why do you want to get lucid in your dreams?

The next step of the Lucidity Quiz is to go back through all the questions and jot down your *ideal* answers. This illuminates your ideal relationship with your sleeping and dreaming mind. It can be very positive to hold an ideal goal lightly in mind as you get more deeply into lucid dreaming. It's nice to revisit this quiz every so often, to see how your sleeping and dreaming life transforms when you pay attention to it, and in order to create a fresh Unique Lucidity Programme.

Best Techniques Based on Your Dreamer Type

Now that you've done the Lucidity Quiz, you'll have a clearer idea of the kind of dreamer and sleeper you are. When we understand this, we can fast-track towards the most effective lucid dreaming techniques for us personally. This helps us avoid wasting time on techniques that likely won't work for us.

Below, you'll see a list of different dreamer or sleeper types. Each type is set up as a Lucidity Programme, with my recommendations for the best path to get lucid and the techniques that are most likely to work well for that particular type. I've pointed to specific practices from this book so you can always refer to this chapter when creating Unique Lucidity Programmes for yourself as your path into lucid dreaming deepens and transforms.

You will identify with more than one type of sleeper/dreamer and will probably fit into quite a few categories. Go through the list below and choose from the fifteen different types. In short, these are: the five-hour sleeper; the deep sleeper; the light sleeper; the agitated sleeper; the insomniac; the high-recall dreamer; the low-recall dreamer; the anxious or depressed dreamer; the highly aware person; the visual and imaginative thinker; the unsupported dreamer; the child-prodigy dreamer; the happy dreamer; the lucid dreamer; and the nightmare sufferer.

It's useful to write down your own unique combination of types. After taking the Lucidity Quiz, one person might identify themselves as "a deep sleeper, nightmare sufferer, visual and imaginative thinker with an upbringing unsupportive of dreams." Another person may describe themselves as "an occasional lucid dreamer, high dream recall, no full-blown nightmares but anxiety present in many dreams, and some insomnia."

There are a large number of possible combinations of sleeper and dreamer types, and not enough space in this book to write a programme for every single combination. Instead, what I've done is provide you with three examples of Unique Lucidity Programmes for common combinations of sleeper /dreamer types (see Appendix II) so you get the idea and can then create your own. You can do this quickly and easily by referring to the listed suggestions for the most effective lucidity techniques for each overall sleeper /dreamer type that you identify with, and combining them into a programme that reflects your individual needs. There's also a Unique Lucidity Programme template in Appendix I for you to fill out with your own tailor-made routine.

Remember that all my suggestions below should only be viewed as guidelines. If a particular practice is recommended for a type of sleeper/dreamer that you don't resonate with, this doesn't mean you shouldn't try that practice! All the practices in *The Art of Lucid Dreaming* can be used by anyone at any time—the aim of the Lucidity Quiz is simply to fast-track you to the best techniques for your specific sleeper/dreamer type.

Your personal Lucidity Programme can and should be changed and expanded on at any time, so it's helpful to keep a record of what works best for you. Never force yourself to continue with a technique that bores or irritates you; gravitate to the ones you find the most inspiring. If the first programme you create isn't optimal for you, throw some different techniques into the mix. Lucidity is closely tied to flexibility and it's always good to experiment with an open mind to discover the combination of techniques that suits you best at this point in your life.

⟨∽ *Lucidity Programme 1* ∽⟩
The Five-Hour Sleeper

If you only sleep around four to five hours a night (as someone who can't function on less than seven hours a night, I shake my head in wonder at how you manage it!), then you would likely do best to forget trying to get lucid at night, unless you remember your dreams each morning.

- Take an afternoon nap so you tumble straight into light, dream-rich REM sleep. This is because your sleep cycle is so short that most of it will be taken up with deep, recuperative sleep, and your REM cycles will be shorter (they get longer as the night goes on). Your brain chemistry will be optimal for lucid dreaming during a nap, so try and squeeze one into your day. Even twenty minutes can be beneficial, recharging and revitalising you, as well as giving you some seriously amazing dream time with a high chance of getting lucid. Combine your nap with *Practice 25: Create a Pre-Sleep Visualisation to Trigger Lucidity.*

- Journal the dreams you have during your naps, as in *Practice 2: Power Up Your Dream Journal.*

- Try a dream re-entry visualisation such as *Practice 21: Dream Reliving.*

- On the weekends, you could also try *Practice 10: Wake Up, Back to Bed.*

❦ *Lucidity Programme 2* ❦
The Heavy Sleeper

You will usually be better off trying to get lucid during an afternoon nap, unless you have a memorable dream cycle at the end of your night of sleep and wake up each morning with dreams in your head.

- Try *Practice 3: Create a Lucid Dream Goal to Fire Up Your Intent to Get Lucid.* It's harder for heavy sleepers to cut through their natural physiological tendencies to get lucid, so you'll need to stoke up your motivation.

- I recommend getting up at your usual time, meditating for five to ten minutes, then returning to bed for half an hour to practise your dozing powers as a good lead-in to a lucid dream so you get used to the feel of floating on the cusp of sleep. This is also a great way of building lucid intent. *See Practice 39: Meditation for Clarity and Lucid Intent.*

- *Practice 10: Wake Up, Back to Bed* helps you to experience a lighter, more alert sleep at a time in your sleep cycle when you are prone to vivid dreaming.

- Combine an afternoon nap with *Practice 25: Create a Pre-Sleep Visualisation to Trigger Lucidity.*

- Sleep elsewhere—when we do this, we tend to have a lighter sleep. See *Practice 19: Sleep Under the Stars... or at Least in a Different Room.*

∽ *Lucidity Programme 3* ∽
The Light Sleeper

Welcome to my kind of sleeping! Light sleepers have an advantage when it comes to lucid dreaming, as we are naturally alert even during sleep.

- I recommend starting with the simple but effective trick that teaches us how to be aware throughout the night. Anchor your intention to become lucid in your dreams to a pebble or other object, then go to sleep with it in your hand and try to keep hold of it all night. This gives you a powerful prompt to help you get lucid in your dreams. See *Practice 24: Create a Lucidity Ritual.*

- Use your body to trigger awareness that you're dreaming, as shown in *Practice 11: Create Your Own Personal Lucidity Trigger.*

- Dream re-entry techniques are also great for this type of sleeper. See *Practice 21: Dream Reliving.*

- Remind yourself during mini-awakenings in the night of your intention to get lucid and learn to glide straight into a lucid dream from there, as in *Practice 15: Use Mini-Awakenings to Cement Your Intent to Get Lucid.*

- Observe your pre-sleep imagery as in *Practice 18: Surfing on the Edge of Sleep.* Light sleepers can become amazing at doing this and it's a fast-track to wake-induced lucid dreams.

∽ *Lucidity Programme 4* ∽
The Agitated Sleeper

If you experience sleep disturbances such as sleepwalking, talking in your sleep, thrashing around, waking up screaming, physically acting out your dreams, or sleep paralysis (where you feel locked in your body and unable to wake up), this can feel bewildering. It can also be disruptive for bed partners.

In terms of getting lucid, the positive thing about having sleep disturbances is that there may be a high level of lucidity (except in night terrors, where people thrash and scream but then carry on sleeping normally, often with zero recall of what happened the next day). Here's how to capitalise on that high lucidity to turn sleep disturbances into beautiful lucid dreams.

- When awake, whenever you experience any negative feelings such as fear, distress, or panic, do a reality check to see if you are dreaming. This will help you to use negative feelings as a lucidity trigger when they happen at night. Revisit *Practice 5: The Five Most Effective Reality Checks.*

- *Practice 58: Sleep Paralysis Tricks* will help you use this state as a springboard into lucid dreaming. In sleep paralysis, the bonus is that you are already lucid—you just need to enable a lucid dream to form around you.

- *Practice 38: The Lucid Writing Technique* and *Practice 54: Changing a Nightmare with Lucid Writing* both enable you to practise changing negative sleep paralysis experiences into fearless lucid adventures. These practices could also help you investigate possible hidden, inner reasons for sleep disturbances, such as repressed fears or past trauma (sleep disturbances are not necessarily linked to these things, but if you discover that they are, please consider seeing a counsellor for support).

  Relax, focus mentally on your recent sleep paralysis experience (or on the feelings of confusion or distress upon waking from a sleep disturbance), and write without stopping to think. Remember that you can stop this process at any point if it becomes painful or upsetting. Another tactic is to write out your ideal reaction to frightening sleep paralysis experiences, such as floating happily into a place of great beauty and meeting some fun people there.

- It's good to create a regular and ongoing pre-sleep meditation practice to clear your thoughts, calm your emotions, and soothe your mind. See *Practice 39: Meditation for Clarity and Lucid Intent* and customise it to suit you.

⚭ *Lucidity Programme 5* ⚭
The Insomniac

If you have trouble falling asleep, or spend hours in the night wide awake, you could put your alertness to good use and simultaneously resolve at least a portion of your insomnia by practising the techniques in chapter 3 on relaxing into lucid dreaming.

- Look out for your pre-sleep imagery and allow it to pull you into a lucid dream, as in *Practice 18: Surfing on the Edge of Sleep.*

- Any type of yoga would be beneficial, including the simplest form, which is lying on your back and focusing on your breath while imagining something peaceful, such as a lucid dream of flying over an enchanting landscape. Try *Practice 25: Create a Pre-Sleep Visualisation to Trigger Lucidity.*

- Let sleeplessness become your gateway to beautiful, restful lucid dream experiences with *Practice 10: Wake Up, Back to Bed.*

- If you wake up in the night and can't get back to sleep and find yourself stressing about things, get out of bed and sit in darkness with zero stimulus until your thoughts calm down. Then return to bed and try *Practice 21: Dream Reliving.*

- Some people take the hormone melatonin for insomnia, but in some cases, this helps us sleep so deeply that we reduce our chances of getting lucid. Do check any medicines, hormones, or stimulants you ingest and consider their effect on your dream life and sleep. Always consult your doctor before making any changes in your medication. *Practice 24: Create a Lucidity Ritual* shows how to combine relaxation with lucid dream incubation to promote a healthy night of sleep.

∽ *Lucidity Programme 6* ∾
The High-Recall Dreamer

Anyone with high dream recall has already taken a big step towards lucid dreaming because you are used to shining conscious attention on your dreams—you just need to remember to apply this attention *during* the dream as well as after it!

- Try *Practice 6: Invent Your Own Unique Reality Check* and get really into questioning your reality in every state of consciousness.

- You will benefit from any of the core techniques in chapter 3, such as *Practice 19: Sleep Under the Stars... or at Least in a Different Room*, or *Practice 23: Hone Your Strangeness Radar*.

- It would be valuable for you to start working with dream re-entry techniques to prime yourself to get lucid. See *Practice 21: Dream Reliving* and *Practice 38: The Lucid Writing Technique*.

∽ *Lucidity Programme 7* ∽
The Low-Recall Dreamer

Don't despair if you rarely recall your dreams. It's possible to change things around!

- Turn yourself into a dreamcatcher and insist on a lie-in at least once a week. The morning is the best moment to float lightly into your dreams and re-emerge with whole scenes fresh in your mind.

- *Practice 18: Surfing on the Edge of Sleep* would be helpful whenever you get a chance to lie down during the day and as you're falling asleep. Keep paper and pen to hand.

- Start to notice the mini-awakenings we all experience multiple times a night and activate yourself to remember what you were just dreaming about. Be prepared to write down what you recall.

- Keep a notepad by your bed and feel determined every night (and during the night whenever you wake up briefly or become aware of turning over in your sleep) to remember something—anything —from your dreams. It can be a colour, a feeling, a sensation such as flying or feeling a snowflake fall onto your cheek. Write it down. See *Practice 2: Power Up Your Dream Journal*.

- Chapter 3 is full of techniques to help you enter the exciting gateway of pre-sleep imagery, and once you've mastered that, lucid dreaming is only moments away. For starters, try *Practice 24: Create a Lucidity Ritual* and *Practice 19: Sleep Under the Stars... or at Least in a Different Room*.

⁶⁄ₒ *Lucidity Programme 8* ₒ⁄⁶
The Anxious or Depressed Dreamer

If you're the kind of dreamer who doesn't usually have full-blown nightmares but finds that anxiety is often present in your dreams, or if you sometimes wake up in the night feeling very anxious, this can indicate underlying anxiety. If you suffer from depression, you may either find that you recall almost no dreams, or that your dreams are very vivid, prolific, and sometimes disturbing. Dreaming can be exhausting for people with anxiety or depression, but the good news is that both issues can be helped by spending more time in deep relaxation during the day.

- Look at all the practices in chapter 3 on relaxing your way into lucid dreaming and pick your favourite. *Practice 17: Shapeshifting* can be delightful to play with while deeply relaxed; and in chapter 5, *Practice 28: Cultivate Serenity* is good for mindfulness and emotional balance.

- *Practice 18: Surfing on the Edge of Sleep* is a wonderful practice for anyone who feels anxious or depressed. See if you can find the sweet spot where you can't feel your body any longer and feel completely warm, well, and content!

- *Practice 56: Ten Nightmare Options for Use in Lucid Imaging and Lucid Dreaming* is a useful reminder of how we can change our reality and re-play our inner movie in healing ways.

- *Practice 57: Anxiety, Unease, and Fear as Lucidity Triggers* can be good for getting you lucid—be sure to read chapter 7 on guiding dreams and also the nightmare chapter before you start using this trigger so you can calmly guide your lucid dream into a healing scenario, or change it to experience anything you want.

- I hear from people who tell me their anxiety medicine makes their dreams go crazy—not necessarily in a good way. Some tell me a particular anti-depressant caused them to have zero dream recall. It's good to pay attention to any medicines you're taking and be aware of the effect they may have on your dreams. Always consult your doctor before making any changes in your medication. Take good care of yourself and send yourself love whenever you can.

⟿ *Lucidity Programme 9* ⟾
The Highly Aware Person

If you already have a high level of mental alertness in waking life and in dreams, and if you regularly assess your current state of consciousness, your enquiring mind and clarity of thought will be of great help in getting lucid in your dreams.

- *Practice 7: Use Your Memory to Get Lucid* along with *Practice 9: The MILD Technique* are useful for highly aware people, especially those who like to take a scientific approach to lucid dreaming. Experiment with different versions of these practices and create your own specific memory jogs to discover the fastest way to remind you to assess your state of consciousness while in the dream state.

- *Practice 6: Invent Your Own Unique Reality Check* will be helpful to you for the same reason.

- Another lovely way of becoming adept at bringing high alertness into a semi-dreaming state is to practise the art of daydreaming. See *Practice 20: Become a Dedicated Daydreamer.*

- You may find it easy to enlist the help of dream people and animals to wake you up in your dreams because your own high mental alertness will permeate your dreams. Try *Practice 31: Get Dream Figures on Your Side.* Also explore *Practice 52: How Conscious Are Your Dream Figures?*

⟿ *Lucidity Programme 10* ⟾
The Visual and Imaginative Thinker

Your dreams are not buried deeply beneath your waking self; they flow right under the surface of your waking imagination. People who are visual thinkers (the apple test from the quiz is a quick way of checking if this means you) are likely to do especially well working with lucid dream induction visualisations and dream re-entries. Chapter 3 explores these.

- It could be helpful for you to take *Practice 36: Talk to Dream People, Objects, and Animals* and rehearse conversations with dream figures in your imagination before trying it in your dreams. When we mentally rehearse an action using visual imagery to reinforce it, we send a strong message to our unconscious mind that this it can (and will!) be done.

- *Practice 25: Create a Pre-Sleep Visualisation to Trigger Lucidity* will be a fun technique for you to get creative with, as will *Practice 17: Shapeshifting*.

- *Practice 40: Musical Trance* could be especially magical for visual thinkers.

- You can draw on your visualisation skills to induce an out-of-body experience if you want to explore this. See *Practice 65: How to Trigger an Out-of-Body Experience from a Lucid Dream and from Waking*.

- Any of the practices that involve lucid imaging should work well for you. Try *Practice 50: A Guide to Successful Lucid Dream Sex* or play with *Practice 55: The Lucid Imaging Nightmare Solution*.

∽ *Lucidity Programme 11* ∽
The Unsupported Dreamer

If your early home life was not supportive of dreams, or actively against dreams, with adults or other authority figures telling you "dreams are nonsense, they aren't real, they're a waste of time, don't bore me with your dreams!" you may need to work harder than others to create new beliefs about the value of dreams. Our beliefs, even when we aren't fully aware of them, can hold us back when we start a lucid dreaming practice.

I often hear from people who are fascinated by the concept of lucid dreaming, but it turns out they have a block about it that they don't understand at first. Others write saying how wonderful they feel lucid dreams are, but their wife thinks they're wasting their time. Even in adulthood we can be unsupported dreamers. Scorn or disapproval from those we are close to can be hurtful and can even stop us from waking up in our dreams.

- In chapter 1, we looked at how to dissolve common blocks around lucid dreaming. Revisit these, and if disapproval is coming from a particular person in your life, it could be helpful to encourage them to discover where their resistance comes from.

- Keeping a dream journal is a good way of honouring your connection with your dreaming mind and reminding yourself of the value of dreams, as in *Practice 2: Power Up Your Dream Journal.*

- *Practice 49: Test Your Belief System* could give you greater insight into any deeply rooted ideas you carry about lucid dreaming.

- Become part of a dreaming community—this is such a powerful and rewarding way of feeling connected to other lucid dreamers and this supportive environment can really spark lucid dreaming. Join an online lucid dreaming forum or a Facebook group, find out about dream groups or workshops in your area—or come on one of my lucid dreaming ocean retreats!

The International Association for the Study of Dreams organises big annual dream conferences which are just wonderful to attend, and IASD also creates regional events. Reach out for support and community, and you'll no longer be an unsupported dreamer.

᥆ᥱᥣ *Lucidity Programme 12* ᥣᥱ᥆
The Child Prodigy Dreamer

If you were a big dreamer as a child and perhaps experienced lucid sleepwalking, lucid flying dreams, or had full-on out-of-body experiences, you have a natural inclination for lucid dreaming. Perhaps you were so connected to your intuition that you always knew who was calling the moment the phone rang or had dreams or nightmares that came true. Maybe you had an inclination towards astonishing consciousness experiences as a child but lost it along the way and want to get it back.

We carry all our younger selves within us; our three-year-old self, our four-year-old self, and so on, right up to the age we are now. It's always possible to reconnect with these younger selves, and our "lost" abilities are never truly lost.

- Find ways back into your child-self. Write your name in tall letters on a sandy beach, find a hill on a blustery day and lean into the wind for that exuberant kick, play cat's cradle, or go to a water park and shriek with wild abandon as you shoot down the slides. Go to sleep with an object, scent, or photograph that reminds you of your childhood.

- Try *Practice 17: Shapeshifting* and imaginatively inhabit the body and mind of your child-self. Go on an adventure! Rediscover your sense of wonder and reclaim the amazing abilities you possessed.

- Use *Practice 38: The Lucid Writing Technique* to reconnect with your child-self. In a light trance, summon a mental image of yourself at a young age, then begin your writing with: "I am five years old…" and let the voice of your child-self tell you stories about how it feels to be that age, what's important, what's upsetting, what scares you, and what sets you free.

- Take your child-self on a fabulous flight of the imagination with *Practice 51: A Guide to Flying in Lucid Dreams*.

✏ *Lucidity Programme 13* ✏
The Happy Dreamer

If you're someone who feels hugely content with your dream life, that's fantastic! If it feels the only thing that's missing is more lucid dreams, it may be good to shake things up a little.

- Sometimes, shaking up our routine can help a happy dreamer to snap into lucidity—try sleeping elsewhere, in a tent in the garden or on your yoga mat in the kitchen. Unfamiliar sleeping environments can trigger lucidity in the cosiest of dreamers. See *Practice 19: Sleep Under the Stars … or at Least in a Different Room*.

- Modify your dream content with a pre-bed movie. Only do this if you think it would be fun—but something to try might be to watch a high-drama soap opera before bed, or even a thriller. This is to encourage different dream content that night.

   Then you set a firm intention to become lucid as soon as you feel a rush of strong emotion … or a wave of uneasiness! Getting lucid should be a fun process, not a scary one, so if you're someone who dislikes thrillers, stick to dramatic soap operas or choose a documentary about penguins and set the intention to get lucid the next time you see a penguin. Be creative and choose a pre-sleep movie that works for you to trigger lucidity. A lucid dreaming YouTube video could also work nicely.

- Work on the hypnagogic, pre-sleep state with *Practice 18: Surfing on the Edge of Sleep*.

- Try the following practices: *Practice 13: Compile a Lucidity Playlist* to break through into your dreams and remind you to do a reality check, and *Practice 14: The Stuck Arm Technique*, to draw you directly into a lucid dream.

⟋⟍ *Lucidity Programme 14* ⟋⟍
The Lucid Dreamer

If you are already a lucid dreamer and are looking to improve your frequency, increase the length of your lucid dreams, or discover new induction techniques, try reading a few pages of a lucid dreaming book before bed each night to cement your intention to get lucid, and experiment with the practices that you haven't come across yet. Lucid dreaming can come in waves, and it's always helpful to read new books by a variety of authors or watch fresh videos on the subject to kick-start your practice again. Explore new techniques and allow these to give you a new angle on lucid dreaming.

- *Practice 23: Hone Your Strangeness Radar* and *Practice 22: Start a Bodywork Practice* can help increase your overall awareness.

- Engage imaginatively with your lucid dreams while awake. Try *Practice 38: The Lucid Writing Technique* to get into playing lucidly with dream material in a creative trance.

- *Practice 55: The Lucid Imaging Nightmare Solution* can be used to spark ideas of inventive ways to interact with dreams. Choose a dream in which you wished you had become lucid and imagine yourself navigating it with lucid awareness.

- To become more adept at having longer, stable lucid dreams, try *Practice 29: Staying Lucid: The CLEAR Technique*.

∽ *Lucidity Programme 15* ∽
The Nightmare Sufferer

We've all woken up terrified from a nightmare, but for some people bad dreams are a regular event. It's heartbreaking when people ask me for help because their nightmares are so terrible that they are scared to fall asleep. What a way to live! I would love to see more people understand that they can harness the incredible power and creative energy of nightmares. Lucid dreaming can help us to do just this. Chapter 8 shows that nightmares can truly be healing gifts—if we allow them to be.

- Nightmare sufferers could do well with pre-sleep meditations and calming pre-sleep rituals. See *Practice 4: Early Morning Meditation to Incubate a Lucid Dream* and *Practice 24: Create a Lucidity Ritual.*

- Immediately upon waking from a bad dream, try *Practice 55: The Lucid Imaging Nightmare Solution* to inspire healing and trigger lucid dreaming.

- Remind yourself of the options—nightmares can be changed with lucidity, either while we're lucid in the dream, or when we wake up and work with them in lucid and imaginative ways. See *Practice 56: Ten Nightmare Options for Use in Lucid Imaging and Lucid Dreaming.*

- Have a shot at *Practice 54: Changing a Nightmare with Lucid Writing*, as this can be a transformative and healing approach to take.

- *Practice 59: How to Relax Around Frightening Dream Figures* should help nightmare sufferers. The main thing to remember is that nightmares come to help us and can be incredibly healing and creative gifts. We can interact with nightmares in beneficial ways when we release our fear.

As your lucidity practice deepens, your sleeper/dreamer type may well change considerably. You might experience much higher dream recall, for example, or no longer be an insomniac or a nightmare sufferer. It's worth revisiting the Lucidity Quiz every so often to check in with yourself, note any changes, and see if you need to revise your current Unique Lucidity Programme by incorporating new techniques for getting lucid.

In Appendix I, there's a blank programme template for you to fill out. In Appendix II, you'll find three example Unique Lucidity Programmes for common combinations of sleeper/dreamer types to give you an idea of how it works. The next practice lays out clear steps for creating your Unique Lucidity Programme.

◌◦◦ *Practice 27* ◦◦◌
How to Create Your Own
Unique Lucidity Programme

The value of creating a tailor-made programme is that it will resonate with you on the deepest levels, mentally, physically, and emotionally. It will suit your personal cognitive style, reflect your unique sleeper/dreamer type, and pique your interest far better than a generalised lucidity programme could.

1. Take the Lucidity Quiz. Spend time and care on it—do it with full lucidity!

2. The list of different sleeper/dreamer types is summarised here: the five-hour sleeper; the heavy sleeper; the light sleeper; the agitated sleeper; the insomniac; the high-recall dreamer; the low-recall dreamer; the anxious or depressed dreamer; the highly aware person; the visual and imaginative thinker; the unsupported dreamer; the child prodigy dreamer; the happy dreamer; the lucid dreamer; and the nightmare sufferer.

3. Read the list and pick the categories you identify with to come up with your own unique combination. For example: "heavy sleeper, nightmare sufferer, visual thinker, low-recall dreamer."

4. Check through the Lucidity Programmes in this chapter that correspond with the categories of sleeper/dreamer types that you fit with. Note down techniques that particularly appeal to you. Go with your intuition when choosing them.

5. If you fall into a large number of sleeper/dreamer categories, choose only those categories that seem particularly strong for you, and whittle down the core practices to a manageable amount: around three.

Save the others for when you come back and refine your Unique Lucidity Programme in the future.

6. Choose your intent-raising practice from this list: Practices 7–10; 15; 19–25; or 39.

7. Choose your three favourite reality checks as in *Practice 5: The Five Most Effective Reality Checks* or create your own using *Practice 6: Invent Your Own Unique Reality Check.*

8. Use the guided template in Appendix I to fill in the programme to suit you personally. Add your pre-sleep routine, your dream journaling goals, and decide on the duration. If you get stuck, check out the three example Unique Lucidity Programmes in Appendix II.

9. Begin your Unique Lucidity Programme tonight!

———————

In this chapter we've worked with the Lucidity Quiz to assess what type of sleeper and dreamer we are. In doing the quiz, we raise our awareness of our dream life and deepen our understanding of ourselves as individual sleepers and dreamers. We've seen how to fast-track our personal route to lucidity by leapfrogging to the induction techniques that suit us best. I've shared the process of how to channel the most effective lucid dream induction techniques for you into a tailor-made Unique Lucidity Programme.

This first section of the book has focused on sharing highly practical tips and techniques for getting lucid in dreams. Now that you've created your Unique Lucidity Programme, the excitement begins as you dedicate yourself to your new routine. In synch with this, it's time to move on to the important next step—how to *stay* lucid in a dream and become adept at stabilising and lengthening lucid dreams. The next chapters examine how to keep our mental focus in the giddying and sometimes overwhelmingly awesome environment of a lucid dream.

PART TWO

Staying Lucid: How to Have Longer, More Satisfying Lucid Dreams

CHAPTER 5

Powerful Practices for
Longer Lucid Dreams

Now that you're equipped with all the best techniques for getting lucid, it's time to move on to the next stage of the journey. Once we've managed to get lucid in a dream, how do we stay lucid? Often, beginner lucid dreamers are so overjoyed and excited when they become lucid that they lose their focus and wake up immediately, kicking themselves for losing a chance to consciously explore their dream world. This part of the book shows what to do once you become lucid in a dream. We'll look in practical terms at how to stabilise lucidity and prolong the experience. The focus is on cultivating mental clarity and calm awareness.

Are you someone who experiences strong emotions every day? Do you swing from wild joy at the beauty of the day to frustration that you have to work late, or go from humming happily under your breath to letting forth a string of expletives when you realise you forgot something important? Do you let people get under your skin and rail at them internally when they upset you? We're only human and it's normal for us to move through a rainbow of emotions in response to daily interactions and events. Many of us actively seek an emotional punch by choosing to watch soap operas and dramas, or by reading passionate, high-stakes novels. Others take things a step further and turn their closest relationships into an emotional rollercoaster, becoming addicted to the highs and lows.

While waking reality isn't going to wobble and dissolve before our eyes when we get sucked into strong emotions, the lucid dream reality can do just that. Dreams tend to involve powerful emotions. Some dreams have the highest of high stakes: we cling to the edge of a cliff by our fingernails, looking down into the waiting jaws of a fire-breathing dragon. Or we realise we have absentmindedly left our baby in a café and when we race back in a panic, he's gone. Or a giant spider with robotic legs climbs through our bedroom window, its fangs glinting …

Fear is a major cause of the loss of dream lucidity, so when we don't know how to handle our own fear, we jeopardise our lucid dreaming practice. Either we wake up in a fright, or we race for our lives and lose lucidity because we get too sucked into the dream. But we can turn this pattern on its head. These days, feeling anxiety, apprehension, stress, or fear in a dream nearly always automatically results in me becoming lucid. This is because I've trained my mind over years to recognise these negative emotions and question my reality when I experience them. Training the mind in this way helps in waking life situations too, by giving us perspective on a situation.

Dreams are so beguiling in their intensity that when we emotionally engage with their high-stakes plots, staying lucidly aware can be tricky to say the least. We get sucked into the dream reality just as we get sucked into our favourite TV drama. This is why it's important to cultivate calmness and serenity in waking life and practise ways of calming down, so that when we get lucid in a dream, we can flick a mental switch and move from terror to calm alertness within moments. When we practise serenity (or at least get better at calming our emotions), we are also practising clarity, the second of the three essential lucidity skills of ICE (intent, clarity, expectation). Let's have a look at how to get more serene in waking life in order to have longer, more stable lucid dreams.

ᖗᖇ *Practice 28* ᖇᖗ
Cultivate Serenity

The more natural it feels to notice and calm our emotions by day, the easier it becomes to do this in a dream.

- During the day, get into the habit of noticing when the tide of emotion in you rises. Pinpoint the moment when one emotion changes into another. You might feel relaxed and balanced at breakfast, then read a message on your phone and instantly feel stressed out. Notice the change without judging it. Staying lucid in dreams relies on noticing when things change: the moment colours fade, or the instant that a gripping event sucks you in, causing your lucid focus to slip.

- Label your emotions: "I'm feeling stubborn now that she's said that." Or: "Those orange flowers dancing in the breeze make me feel so happy!" Or: "My temper is really rising now."

- Experiment with ways of calming down during the day. Whenever you notice you're angry, sad, fearful, or anxious, take deep breaths and imagine yourself in your dream body, perhaps floating a little, successfully staying calm and curious while the dream unfolds around you. View waking life events as a dream—how would you react to this situation if it was a dream?

- Use the TV to help you get lucid: whenever you're watching the box and something really gripping happens that totally enthrals you, do a reality check! Yes, even when your favourite football team is about to score the winning goal, or when a soap opera heroine is breathing her last breath … ride on that tide of emotion, but stay lucid! Check your state of consciousness. Ask yourself if this is a dream.

- Create an affirmation that works for you in waking life and prepare to use it in your dreams. "I am peaceful and relaxed." "Everything is unfolding for the greatest possible good." "I am alert and curious to whatever comes next." Smile confidently as you think it.

- Link your affirmation to a physical gesture, such as making an "O" shape with your lips and breathing out slowly to release excess emotion, or clapping your hands to snap yourself into a calmer mindset.

Use this gesture in your dreams to stay calm and lucidly aware, even when fearful events are afoot.

- When things get seriously scary in a dream, use your calming techniques and remind yourself firmly: "This is a *dream*. I will wake up safely in my bed after this experience. *I am safe*." Teach yourself to observe lucid dream scenes and events with a curious, fearless attitude.

Once we're used to being lucid in our dreams, it's possible to experience all manner of incredibly exciting or scary situations and remain fully lucid. People can experience mind-blowing orgasms and not lose lucidity, or enjoy an exhilarating swoop on an eagle's back without the excitement catapulting them awake. The most terrible nightmare images can be faced in a lucid dream without people's initial fear waking them up, because reminding themselves that this is a dream removes much of their fear within seconds. This fearless lucid engagement with frightening dream images often leads to spontaneous healing and insight. In the beginning, though, we need to be able to calm down on cue and activate our lucid mindset in order to prolong the lucid dream.

The Stages of Lucidity

The thing to remember about lucid dreaming is that we aren't just talking about one level of mental alertness; there are varying stages of lucidity. Put another way, lucidity is all about *awareness*, and this awareness has different levels of intensity. Think about the way that sometimes during the day we are super-alert and focused. We get our work done in a flash, or play a ball game with supreme concentration. At other moments, we feel sluggish and unfocused. We make simple mistakes because even though we're awake, we're not alert.

It's the same in the dream state. Lucid awareness can be thought of as a light switch with a dimmer function. In some non-lucid dreams, the dimmer switch is turned down to its lowest setting. Our thinking is muddled. We lurch from one emotion to the next and we accept ridiculous situations unquestioningly ("I am being chased by a three-headed monster." "I am the first woman on Jupiter.") The brighter the light becomes, the more lucid and clear-thinking we become in our dreams. We begin to question the reality we find ourselves in. We come up with logical arguments and think creatively. When the light of awareness shines brightly enough, we experience that magical moment of realisation: "Wow—I'm dreaming right now!" But even within lucid dreams, our awareness can be dimmer or brighter. Let's look at the stages of lucidity more closely to see how this affects our dream experience.

Deeply Non-Lucid

We have zero awareness of this being a dream. Instead, we blindly accept the craziest situations, such as being captain of a sinking cruise liner or being attacked by a dinosaur.

Non-Lucid but Alert

Although we don't recognise that we're dreaming, we are capable of reasoning logically throughout the dream, and our choices and actions are close to those we would choose while awake.

Pre-Lucid

We may question the reality of the dream, or even carry out a reality check to see if this is a dream, yet reach the conclusion that we are awake … only to wake up and discover that we were in fact dreaming!

Lucid but Overexcited

This is a classic rookie mistake that causes frustration for many beginner lucid dreamers. We become lucid in a dream but are so excited to be awake in the dream world that we lose our focus and wake up immediately, feeling frustrated that we've messed up the opportunity.

Lucid but Struggling

Staying lucid is an art all its own, which is why two chapters of this book are dedicated to this topic. Sometimes it's hard to retain full lucid awareness. Typically, we get swept up in the emotion and actions of the dream and lose lucidity, or attempt to fly and have trouble getting off the ground. In a single dream, our lucid awareness can be high, shaky, or low. We need to learn the art of mental focus in order to stabilise the dream.

Lucid and Stable

This is a fun level of lucid dreaming, because we are able to carry out actions in the dream, guide events, or simply go with the flow while remaining lucidly aware. It may occasionally be necessary to stabilise the dream or remind ourselves to stay lucid.

Lightbulb Bright Lucid

Lucidity is clear, strong, and effortless. It's as easy as staying awake during the waking state, so it's a fantastic basis for exploring, experimenting, and adventuring. Long lucid dreams can be experienced, sometimes lasting an hour or more. Rarely, people even report staying lucid all night long, even through the deepest, imageless stages of sleep.

Lucid Light

This is the holy grail of lucid dreaming because of its spiritual and philosophical treasures. In this state, we are effortlessly lucid, the dream imagery often tends to dissolve, and we float bodiless in light of any colour or zoom through limitless space. We become lucid on every level and experience blissful oneness. There's nothing quite like it!

These stages of lucidity are only for guidance—explore for yourself and you may find others. There are other lucid states that can be challenging, such as sleep paralysis, where we remain lucid while our body falls asleep, but feel stuck and unable to move. This is due to the natural muscular paralysis we all experience every time we fall asleep, but it can be frightening until we learn how to navigate it. There are tips regarding this in chapter 8 on nightmares.

The speed at which we shift from one stage of lucid awareness to the next can be gradual, but it can also be astonishingly fast. It's possible to go from deeply non-lucid to lightbulb bright lucid in a single second. This often happens when something scary or odd jolts us into understanding that our situation is so impossible that we must be dreaming; with a shock, we become fully lucid. The speed of the change of lucidity is a great thing, because it means that *we can quickly influence our own level of lucidity.*

We can perform specific techniques such as the ones in this chapter and the next to raise our level of awareness from 50 to 100 percent when we feel ourselves losing lucidity. Once we're used to activating these techniques in the dream state, we can maintain lucidity for much longer periods and enjoy long, stable lucid dreams.

What Does It Feel like to Lose Lucidity in a Dream?

Imagine you've just become lucid standing knee-deep in a snowfield. It's dazzling. The snow sparkles with tiny crystals and it's incredibly realistic. You leap around whooping with delight, then reach down with your bare hand and scoop up a little snow to examine it, remembering that in the waking state, every snowflake is unique. Is this true of dream snowflakes? As you're inspecting the intricate structure of one snowflake, you notice it's not melting on your hand, and this makes you smile—the dream world, as realistic as it is, has overseen this detail tonight.

Of course, as soon as you think about it not melting, the snowflake obligingly melts, only it does this at super-fast speed, as if making up for lost time. This makes you laugh and laugh, giddy with the joy of being lucid in this dream. But as you laugh, you notice that everything around you seems to be juddering slightly. What's this? The white glare of the snow is less fierce, more like the dull white of old lace curtains. The vibrancy of the scene is fading by the millisecond and it dawns on you that if you don't act fast, this glorious winter wonderland will simply vanish.

Raising your hands to your face, you look closely at them, noticing they are strangely elongated and thin. "I am lucid," you remind yourself firmly, and now you glance around at the snowy scene again. Sure enough, it's growing brighter again, but before you can stabilise the scene completely, you're distracted by something over to your left that looks like a giant marble swirling with colours. It's big—about the size of a gyroscope—and a wizened man with a stick is tapping it to keep it moving along. Astonished, you watch as it rolls towards the centre of the snowfield like an oversized psychedelic peach.

Your jaw drops—*woah, this is super unexpected, what's going on?*—and suddenly there's a buzzing in your ears and the snowy scene wobbles and collapses, the colourful marble disappears... it's too late to stop it now; you feel yourself rising from sleep, you feel the duvet heavy on your body and your eyes flick open despite themselves. You're awake.

Cool lucid dream—shame it finished so soon! You find yourself thinking, "If only I had stabilised the dream as soon as I became lucid, and only *then* begun to explore. If only I hadn't let the arrival of that giant marble distract me from my lucid dream stabilisation attempts. If only I had calmed myself down instead of laughing too hard and then getting sucked into my own astonishment. If only, if only…" But there's never much point in berating ourselves when this sort of thing happens (and it will, many times). It's more helpful to feel pleased that we got lucid, and take a moment to write down our dream, draw the main images, and rediscover the original imagery created by our very own dreaming mind.

Finally, we can replay the lucid dream in our head, modifying it to insert the lucidity stabilisation techniques we needed and imaginatively allow the dream to continue with us lucidly aware. What happens next? Does the giant marble crack open to reveal a goddess? Or does it steamroll you flat into the snow? It's your call!

Losing lucidity doesn't always have to be a struggle—sometimes we rise naturally from a lucid dream into waking, which can feel very beautiful. Other times, especially at the end of a lengthy lucid dream, we simply let go of our lucidity. Often, we don't even notice ourselves losing lucidity—we simply get sucked into the dream action and emotions and forget all about being lucid. It's only when we wake up that we think back and realise, "Oh, I guess I lost lucidity right after the pirate ship started to sink." The good news is there are ways of creating a clear-focused, steady, lucid mindset, just the kind we need when we're navigating the crazy and beguiling world of dreams.

This book has a strong focus on how to create a lucid mindset with techniques designed to strengthen your alertness and your ability to stay calm and clearheaded in the midst of chaos. There are also many practices in this chapter and the next to help you to stabilise and prolong the dream.

When I started to research lucid dreaming at university in the '90s, at first I didn't have a handbook to help me explore lucid dreaming. I made many mistakes and kicked myself a thousand times for losing lucidity right in the middle of a wonderful dream. I experimented tirelessly with ways of getting and staying lucid and taught myself to lucid dream at will. During the first year, I had about 150 lucid dreams. The year after that, I was lucid nearly every night. I learned how to have long, stable lucid dreams and carried out many experiments on the nature of dream reality, the dream body, dream control, and the creative possibilities of lucid dreaming, making surprising discoveries. Here is my CLEAR lucidity stabilisation technique that I developed in the '90s.

ᥫ᭰ *Practice 29* ᥫ᭰
Staying Lucid: The CLEAR Technique[9]

1. **Calm** down. It can be hard not to be bowled over by the intense realisation that you are awake inside a dream, so the most important thing to do first to avoid losing lucidity is to calm down. Practise ways of calming strong emotions while you're awake. Taking a deep yoga breath helps, as does relaxing the belly by placing a hand on it and counting to three. Find a way that works for you and bring this into the dream state.

2. **Look** around. When you're calm (and while you're calming yourself), look around you. Look at the dream scene, move your eyes, and engage with the dream by noticing detail. This will sharpen your awareness. Many people find that if they fix their gaze for too long on an object in a dream, they wake up, so keep your eyes moving curiously over what you see. Look at your hands briefly (no staring!) and then shift your gaze to the dream scene, then look at your hands again, and so on, until your surroundings are super-clear.

3. **Engage** with the dream. It's vital to engage with the lucid dream. Movement stimulates the conscious brain, so touching a dream wall or stroking a dream leaf is a great way of maintaining lucid awareness. Stamp your dream feet or rub your dream hands together. Engage your senses: listen to someone speaking, smell a dream flower, or jump in the air to feel the floatiness. If being more active helps, then keep on the move: walk, fly, do a sky somersault, or bounce like an astronaut. Discover what works best for you.

---

9. This material previously appeared in *Llewellyn's Complete Book of Lucid Dreaming*.

4. **Announce** that this is a dream. Use a helpful affirmation, such as one of these: "I am lucid." "This is a dream." "Everything in this dream is clear." "Lucidity is easy." If you feel the dream is becoming unstable, this can also take the form of a command, such as "Clarity now!" Make such announcements with great conviction and fully expect them to have the desired result. You can also narrate (out loud or in your head) what you see or what you're doing to help you keep your focus. Remember to use the word "dream" a lot so you don't get so caught up in the imagery that you forget you're dreaming: "I'm standing on top of my house and there are purple-bellied dream clouds above me. Oh wow, a lucid dream bird just appeared and it's got wings made out of string…"

5. **Recall** what you'd like to do. Once you are calm and have made your affirmation, it's a good time to recall your dream goal. What would you like to do? Fly above the Mississippi River? Grow a long, winding arm? Stand and admire the dream in all its splendour? Keep your goal lightly in your mind to focus your awareness. Once you are calm and fully engaged with the dream, anything is possible.

It's helpful to remember these five simple steps and be ready to swing into action with them as soon as you become lucid in a dream: Calm down; Look around; Engage with the dream; Announce "I am lucid"; and Recall your dream goals. These steps might happen in the space of a few seconds, but if it seems hard to maintain lucidity, they could take longer. This is fine—if it doesn't work immediately, return to the first step of calming down. In your first attempts at stabilising a lucid dream, try not to get too hung up on carrying out your dream goal, as this will probably result in you losing lucidity and waking up too soon. The main thing is to get used to creating a stable platform of awareness so the world of lucid dreaming really can become your oyster.

It is deeply amazing simply to look with a conscious gaze at the inner landscape of your unconscious. What a marvel! Touch your dream, soak it up with your lucid gaze, and be present to the lightness of your dream body. You may find that the dream air has a slightly liquid quality, or that even the lowliest object seems to shine with living, conscious awareness. Notice the incredible responsiveness of the imagery as it reacts to your thoughts, expectations, and intentions. See those colours? Such vibrancy! You are the lucid dream, and it is you. This is an awesome state of consciousness, so why not get adept at making it last as long as possible?

Eight More Ways to Stay Lucid

Below, I share eight of my top tips for stabilising lucid dreams. Most of these are techniques to be used while lucid in a dream, and it's a good idea to try them out at your leisure and see which ones work best for you. This first one is a waking practice to increase your powers of observation and turn you into a Sherlock Holmes type who always rapidly solves the mystery, "Am I dreaming now?"

☞ *Practice 30* ☜
Spot the Difference

An experimental, scientific, and observant frame of mind can help us no end to become conscious in our dreams. Think of yourself as a dream detective!

- Make a list of the differences between your non-lucid and lucid dreams. Is there a difference in the vibrancy of the colours, or in your level of logical thinking? Does everything feel ultra-real? Does your mood change? Do your lucid dreams have different themes, storylines, and symbols from those you experience in your less conscious dreams?

- Get specific. Think about every aspect of your dreams, from the air temperature to the density of your dream body. Create an intention to do some simple experiments next time you get lucid, such as seeing if you can put your hand through a wall or testing the precise weight of your dream feet on the ground. Do you tend to skim along without really touching the floor? Remind yourself to look at how (or if) the sun casts shadows in your dreams. Aim to explore the laws of physics, test the way gravity behaves, and dedicate yourself to noticing every detail of your dream world.

- Note any differences between the dream figures that you meet in lucid versus non-lucid dreams. How do the interactions differ? Are you meeting more animals when lucid? How about "Wise Mentor" type dream figures? Some people find that once they begin to get lucid on a regular basis, these figures start showing up more.

- Keep adding to your list of differences. This will help you to build up a clear picture of your dream life as well as honing your awareness so that the next time you are dreaming, you simply recognise the dream for what it is.

- Be scientific and precise. Resolve to notice even more differences and carry out new experiments the next time you get lucid. This is another way of sharpening your mental clarity and getting into the habit of noticing everything. Nothing escapes the lucid you!

⟩⟩ *Practice 31* ⟨⟨
Get Dream Figures on Your Side

One thing to beware of is the uncanny ability of dream figures to distract us from staying lucid. Some even do their utmost to stop us from getting lucid. They might argue with us that this is definitely *not* a dream and make us feel like idiots for even wondering! These figures could be viewed as the part of us that has doubts about the value of lucid dreaming, so if you find this happening it might help to work on dissolving any unhelpful assumptions, doubts, fears, and mental blocks you may have around getting lucid, as explained in chapter 1.

The good news is that dream figures can be amazingly helpful once we get them on our side. In non-lucid dreams, I've had people wink at me and say, "Well, this *is* a dream, so ..." and then they wait with a twinkle in their eye for me to get it and become lucid! Other times, the cue is subtler. A fireman might shimmy part way up a ladder and then fly the rest of the way, laughing down at me until I understand that he's showing me this is a dream. Other times, dream figures only have to give me a certain look of power and presence for me to realise that I'm dreaming. Dream animals show up for me very often in this way, appearing before me and fixing me with a conscious gaze that instantly catapults me into lucidity. Whenever I see anyone practising yoga or other energy work in a dream, this gets me lucid fast. Sometimes dream objects morph under my eyes to show me this is a dream. It's up to us to act on lucidity cues like these and not let them slip past unnoticed.

We can enlist the help of dream figures in getting and staying lucid by treating them respectfully in all our dreams, and by actively asking for their help either in the lucid dream itself, or before we go to sleep at night. Lie down, relax, and reach out mentally with strong intent to all the people, animals, landscapes, and dream objects you'll meet in your dreams that night. Call out to them: "Please help me to get lucid. Show me that I'm dreaming! Thank you." Gratitude is a strong way of sealing intent. Remember to comb through your dreams the next morning to see who or what tried to help you get lucid that night and send them thanks if they did.

⟋⟍ *Practice 32* ⟍⟋
Shift Your Gaze

Sometimes lucid dreams have a disconcerting habit of dissolving if we stare at something for too long. Some people even use staring as a technique to wake themselves up when they're ready to end the dream. When the lucid dream is stable, there's no need to think about keeping your eyes moving around the scene, but if you feel lucidity slipping and the dream growing faint around the edges or trembling, that's the time to remember to flick your gaze around. Avoid prolonged eye contact with a dream figure if you feel lucidity slipping. Instead, allow your lucid gaze to alight on different objects; glance up at the stars and then down at a pebble. Allow your concentration to vamp up as you're doing this to sharpen the dream and restore stability. It can feel astonishing, as if your conscious gaze is stitching the dream scene back together again.

⟋⟍ *Practice 33* ⟍⟋
Spin like a Whirling Dervish

When you feel lucidity slipping away and the dream is dissolving in tatters around you, some lucid dreamers say that spinning your whole body around on the spot can result in the creation of a new, stable dream scene. Give it a whirl and see how it works out for you, but I have to say that for me, this technique tends to result in the entire dream scene vanishing and I am left floating in black space. This is fine with me, because the "lucid void" is a state of vast creative potential and deep peace, and I've grown very familiar with it and its unexpected treasures over the years. Any lucidity practice may have a different effect for different people, and testing techniques with an open mind is the best way to create your own Unique Lucidity Programme.

⚬⚬ *Practice 34* ⚬⚬
Give Yourself a Hand

Hands are great, aren't they? So useful—even in a lucid dream. Here are five ways our hands can help us to stay lucid:

1. Rubbing your hands together can help you to be present in your lucid dream body and focus your attention to stabilise the dream.

2. Clapping can raise your level of mental focus.

3. Trying to put your fingers through the palm of your other hand can be an effective reality check. This quick confirmation that we are dreaming raises our awareness.

4. Touching anything in the dream solidifies its presence and you'll notice this stability spreading to other elements of the dream as well.

5. The simple act of remembering to find your hands in a dream is one of the best-known lucidity triggers, and it's also a useful dream stabilisation technique.

This last technique appeared in the books of Carlos Castaneda[10] in the '60s. It certainly worked for me to find my hands in my dreams when I was deep into my lucidity explorations at university. I used to raise them before my face and try to remain unfazed by the fact they often looked nothing like my actual hands (translucent, or huge and furry). Then I'd use them to stabilise the dream by lifting my gaze to the dream scene and noticing every detail before looking back at my hands. I'd repeat this until the lucid dream was rock solid. Then I'd go and play in it.

Try setting an intention to find your hands in your dreams tonight, and then use your hands in all these different ways to test your reality and stabilise your lucid dream. Let's put our hands together for hands!

⚬⚬ *Practice 35* ⚬⚬
Activate Your Brain with Mental Arithmetic

Even if mathematics isn't your thing, doing a few simple sums in a lucid dream can really boost your mental alertness and result in a nice, bright, sta-

---

10. Castaneda, *Journey to Ixtlan*.

ble dream environment. Even though a tiny percentage of whiz kids successfully use their lucid dreams to work out complex equations or create computer code, for most of us it's best to keep the math simple, because it takes a lot more concentration to juggle numbers in a lucid dream than it does by day. If you attempt something too complex, you risk forgetting all about staying lucid and disappearing (non-lucidly) down a mathematical wormhole. Try something like 7x7=49 or branch out into simple addition such as 9+5=14. This wakes up your brain and increases your awareness.

∽ *Practice 36* ∽
Talk to Dream People, Objects, and Animals

People, objects, and animals are vital parts of the dream and interacting with them can simultaneously raise our lucidity and teach us a great deal about ourselves and our dream world.

- Whenever the lucid dream seems sparser and less vibrant, get sociable. It doesn't matter if there's nobody there—turn and talk to a tree root or strike up a conversation with a skyscraper. This can be a wonderful way both to sharpen your lucid focus and to discover more about your dream images, people, and animals.

- Ask, "Do you have a message for me?" Or "What do you represent?"

- Alternatively, you could chat them up with an honest compliment. You might remark to a dream mouse, "You have such noble whiskers!" Talking to who or what we encounter in our lucid dreams connects us more strongly with the dream and it can be fascinating to hear any responses that come our way.

- Even inanimate objects can speak in lucid dreams if we give them a chance. A caring question such as, "How does it feel to be a USB stick/a brick/a bath tub?" could prompt these objects to pour their hearts out to you.

- If you're less of a talker and more of a strong, silent type, or if you don't want a dream brick sobbing on your shoulder, just stick out your tongue and lick the dream! Seriously, I know a guy called Robin who regularly uses this trick to stabilise his lucid dreams. In one lucid dream, he's on a bus: *"I figure I'll solidify the dream and start licking at random places in the bus. The flavour is really strong, and I can keep that sensation with me which makes the dream feel immortal."* How cool is that?

- Rehearse encounters with dream figures and dream objects by taking a previous dream and writing out dialogue or practising with a friend. (That's if you can find one willing to go along with your harebrained scheme by pretending to be a rainbow butterfly or a rusty bicycle.) Or try this as a pre-sleep, lucidity-inducing visualisation. Rehearsal is a powerful force in the lucid dreaming game because it combines intent and visualisation with the expectation of success.

⚭ *Practice 37* ⚭
Remind Yourself that You Are Lucid in a Dream!

Reminding yourself of your own lucidity may sound weird, but since dreams are so compelling, it can be all too easy to forget that we're in a dream.

- Repeat a lucidity-enhancing mantra whenever you feel the need: "I'm lucid in this dream, lucid in this dream …" Set it to a tune and sing it if this helps. Singing can be a powerful force in lucid dreams, reverberating around the scene with intensity and creating a beautiful energy.

- Pick up an object in the dream: a piece of tree bark, a can of paint, whatever's handy. Keep hold of it as you continue to explore the dream, making sure to squeeze it or glance at it (or lick it!) to remind you that *this is a dream*.

- Create an original lucidity reminder by intending to find one in your pocket (or on the crown of your head) and reaching for it. This can cause wonderful surprises to appear, such as a golden bean or a tiny parrot (just train it to keep squawking "This is a dream!" and staying lucid will be a doddle).

———————

In this chapter, we've examined the beguiling nature of dreams and the importance of counterbalancing this by learning to calm our emotions when we first get lucid and perform various techniques if we feel lucidity slipping.

We've explored lucid awareness as a kind of light switch with a dimmer function, something that has varying stages and intensities. I've shared my CLEAR stabilisation technique and a variety of other practices that combat the loss of lucidity and contribute valuable skills for staying lucid in dreams.

We've also looked at the importance of honing our powers of observation during the day to sharpen our mental clarity. The more we get used to being highly alert in our waking lives, the easier it is to snap into a state of high lucidity in our dreams. The next chapter provides more practices for staying lucid and focuses on how we can use waking trance, creative states, and meditation to train our brains to keep on lucid dreaming.

CHAPTER 6

Train Your Mind to Keep On Lucid Dreaming

The mind is vast and incredibly potent. In some ways it's like a muscle, because the more we use it the stronger it becomes. Lucid dreaming helps us flex our mental "muscles" by using sharp focus and conscious awareness while we're asleep. In becoming adept lucid dreamers, we can put to good use the mind's natural ability to enter "the zone," a highly focused and creative state of consciousness. We can train ourselves to reach and maintain this state of heightened awareness, logical thought, and open-mindedness in dreams, to the point that it becomes habit. We see the results of this training in the length of our lucid dreams and in the rock-solid stability of the dream.

People tell me they are amazed at how natural it feels to be super-aware in a dream where lucidity feels effortless. These count among my favourite types of lucid dreams because mental energy isn't needed to stabilise the dream and is freed up for other adventures and discoveries; I can really relax into my explorations and my level of logical thinking is sky-high and stands up to scrutiny when I examine it after the dream. In one lucid dream, I took a philosophical theory about the minimal input we need to identify with an ego-self, and tested it by systematically reducing my sensory input, "switching off" my sight, olfactory and gustatory senses, hearing, and physical sensations, and then worked on eliminating my sense of existing in space.

At lower levels of lucidity, what we consider to be a logical thought process may sometimes be based on false assumptions, or become slightly muddled, but we may only realise this once we wake up. In one lucid dream, I took paper and pen to copy down a luminous dream tree that I wanted to show others when I woke up—only to realise my mistake moments later and lay it aside, realising (duh!) my drawing won't be there when I wake up from this dream! Within a single dream, lucidity may rise and fall and rise again.

Effortless lucidity can and does happen spontaneously, but many people have to work on raising their consciousness in order to enjoy lengthy, stable lucid dreams. How can we work with the natural power of our mind so that staying lucid in a dream is an expected and effortless outcome? This chapter explores more tricks and tips for prolonging dream lucidity, with its main focus on three powerful methods for training ourselves to stay lucid:

1. Experiment with *creative lucid trances* to simulate lucid dreaming. This trains us to become adept at balancing conscious awareness and unconscious imagery.
2. Increase mental clarity and focus through lucid-dreaming-based meditation, music, and mantras.
3. Practise simple yoga poses to ground ourselves in a dream and increase our mental balance and powers of concentration.

With the practices in this chapter, we continue to bring the forces of intent, clarity, and expectation (ICE) into our lives. ICE can be thought of like physical ice. Imagine a frozen lake. If the ice is thin, it'll shatter when we skate on it. Similarly, if our ICE is not solid, even if we do get lucid, we'll likely wake up instantly because we won't have that solid lucid mindset keeping the dream (and ourselves) steady. The more we bring the principles of ICE into our lives, the more solid our lucid dreaming base becomes, so we can create a reliable surface from which to launch ourselves into lucid dreaming.

Intent, clarity, and expectation are vital forces for lucid dreaming. They prime our mind to get and stay lucid. When we cultivate waking life lucidity and do reality checks at odd moments during the day, we invite focused lucidity into our daily lives. Let's start by diving into the world of creative lucid trances.

Creative Lucid Trances

When we enter a creative lucid trance, we effectively shift our state of consciousness closer to that of our dreaming mind. This is a great skill that helps us to effortlessly extend our lucid dreaming because we get comfortable maintaining a balance between mental alertness and dream imagery. It's also a wonderful state of consciousness in its own right, leading to original ideas and inventive thoughts and imagery.

When I was writing my first novel, *Breathing in Colour*, as part of my doctoral research into lucid dream creativity, I entered lucid trances to develop my ideas about the novel. This is not a deep trance—we are aware that we're in a trance yet our awareness doesn't cause the trance to rupture. We remain in our creative flow, interacting with vivid inner imagery and emotions. It's very dreamlike, very lucid. Many creative writers and artists cherish the creative trance. Stephen King refers to it as "a semi-dreaming state."[11]

There's plenty of overlap between lucid trances and lucid dreaming. In lucid dreams we are physically *asleep* but awake in terms of awareness and mental thought processes. In lucid trances we are physically *awake* but our mental functioning drifts closer to dreaming thought and our awareness bathes in the dreamlike imagery that emerges. It's the marvellous balance between waking and dreaming consciousness in both states that can result in such wild creativity and originality.

We can teach ourselves to enter creative lucid trances. In 2003, I formalised the technique I'd been using for many years and began teaching it. I call it "Lucid Writing."[12] It's simple: in a relaxed state, we re-enter a dream by bringing it to mind in vivid detail, then write without stopping, allowing actions and imagery to develop spontaneously. If we want to guide events, we can pick a previous dream and finish it any way we like in the lucid trance or return to it many times and keep changing the ending. By working

---

11. Epel, *Writers Dreaming*, 141.

12. Johnson, "Lucid Dreaming and the Creative Writing Process."

with a mixture of conscious awareness and unconscious imagery by day, we enhance our ability to stay lucid in our dreams.

The more often we enter creative lucid trances, the more we train our mind to balance comfortably between waking and dreaming. This is similar to the idea behind techniques such as brainwave biofeedback, which improve stress responses by helping people to consciously create brain states that encourage relaxation and creativity. Lucid Writing trains our mind to be alert yet relaxed enough to *continue* conscious dreaming.

Here's the full-detail version of this core practice, complete with golden light visualisation.

⟲⟳ *Practice 38* ⟲⟳
The Lucid Writing Technique[13]

1. Before you begin, consider which dream you'd like to focus on. It's best to choose something vivid and emotional. Focus on one core image rather than a long, convoluted plot. Not only lucid dream imagery but any vivid dream imagery is perfect as a lead-in to Lucid Writing. Dreams are our very own personalised mental imagery, and they are often emotionally charged and radiant.

2. Have a pen and notepad close to hand. Sit comfortably on a sofa or armchair. Close your eyes and keep them closed throughout the next steps.

3. Breathe calmly and deeply several times, then let your breath rise and fall in its own natural rhythm. Observe the breath moving in and out like the ocean breathing.

4. Inhale deeply, and as you do so, turn your head to the right. As you exhale, allow your head to move slowly back to the centre. Inhale as you turn your head to the left. As you exhale, your head returns to the centre. Do this combined breathe-and-head movement for a while, then return your head to the centre and relax.

5. Visualise golden light cascading slowly over your body from head to toe. Consciously relax each part of your body as the light bathes it … head, shoulders, chest, belly, hips, legs, and feet. Focus all your

---

13. This material previously appeared in *Llewellyn's Complete Book of Lucid Dreaming*.

thought and energy on making this bath of light come to life. Allow any unrelated thoughts to drift past without grasping on to them.

6. When you are completely bathed in golden light, create a space in your mind—a luminous, golden space.

7. Now bring your chosen dream image into this golden space. Feel it come alive with emotions, colours, and sensations. Your dream image may move and transform into something else, and you can let this happen. Stay with the flow of imagery as long as you like.

8. When you feel ready, open your eyes slightly, take up your pen, and write without stopping, without caring about spelling or punctuation, and without judging what you write. Simply let it flow out without analysing it. You might find yourself writing about a waking life memory, or extending and changing the dream story. All this is good; let the writing go wherever it goes. If you get stuck, simply return mentally to your dream imagery and continue to write without stopping until you feel you are done.

9. If you prefer to do a variation that doesn't involve writing, continue with the medium of your choice: collaging, doodling, or speaking your observations aloud into a recording device.

In the semi-dreaming state of the creative lucid trance, we combine relaxation, dreams, awareness, and writing. Staying in the trance can take skill and a certain mindset, just as staying lucid in a dream can. Irritating noises like cars roaring past the window, or intrusions like the phone ringing, can eject us from our internal focus. It's important to keep writing even if something distracts us—even if it feels as if we suddenly have nothing to say! Simply write: "I can't think of anything to write," and by the time you've written that, something else will have come into your mind.

The mind is endlessly busy—if you've tried meditation, you'll know how hard it is *not* to think, worry, or create complicated scenarios and list "to-do" actions in your head. So keep your pen moving. If something happens that physically stops us from writing (like having to get up to answer the doorbell), re-reading what we've written helps, or closing our eyes and re-entering the dream from the beginning, focusing our intent as we allow the imagery to come to life again. The one situation where it's best to stop writing is if something traumatic comes up in your writing that you find hard to face. Stop writing and talk to a friend or therapist.

Lucid Writing can result in surprising insights into our dreams. Although at first I taught it purely as a creativity technique, I quickly realised from the reactions of people in my workshops that it can also be a powerful healing tool. Lucid Writing allows us to guide and interact with unconscious dream imagery in intuitive ways, without fear dominating our responses (since we know this is "just a light trance" that we can snap out of any time). The lack of fear and the sense that we are co-creating the imagery can generate unexpected twists in the dream story and result in deep healing. One woman explored a plane crash nightmare in her Lucid Writing and because she was able to re-live the scene without fear, she managed to take charge of the plane and land safely. She emerged with the startling insight that she had been feeling so victimised in her life (she was being bullied at work) that she was set on a crash course, and that she needed to act immediately to take charge, save herself, and be happy again.

Just as in lucid dreams, we can either guide the action in Lucid Writing, or allow it to develop spontaneously before our conscious gaze. The more we practise the internal balance of creative lucid trances, the more adept we become at re-entering the trance if we come out of it too soon, and similar skills are needed for maintaining lucidity in a dream.

Lucid-Dreaming-Based Meditation

We can increase our mental clarity and focus through lucid-dreaming-based meditation, mantras, and music. These waking practices have double power because the more we focus on something while awake, the more likely we are to dream of it … and recognise that we are dreaming right now! Whenever we link a waking activity to the strong intention to become lucid in a dream, we are doing ourselves a big favour and paving the way for a higher frequency of lucid dreams. Meditation is an excellent tool for increasing mental clarity and our ability to stay focused and alert—valuable skills that build our lucid mindset and help us to stay lucid in a dream. Here are the steps for a strong lucid-dreaming-based meditation practice.

ᏈᎧᏍᎧ *Practice 39* ᏟᎧᎦᎧ
Meditation for Clarity and Lucid Intent

The breath is the fastest and most direct route to the self. Take a deep, conscious belly-breath now and see for yourself. Conscious breathing instantly has an effect on our mind and body: our brain is refreshed with extra oxygen, our belly muscles relax, our heart rate slows, and our shoulders release tension. As we continue to take slow, deep breaths, our thoughts grow less hectic; we gain mental clarity, drop excessive thoughts and scenarios, and gradually begin to drift towards a light trance.

Breathing is a fabulous stabilising technique, both in waking life (to calm our emotions and help us to relax and ground ourselves in the present moment) and in lucid dreams. Breathwork is an integral part of any good meditation practice and can be incorporated either at the start of meditation, to centre us and calm our mind, or it can be used throughout the meditation, in synch with a mantra.

- Sit comfortably and close your eyes. Take slow, deep breaths and feel your mind and body become more relaxed and freer. Each time you breathe in, slowly turn your head to the right, breathing slowly out as your head returns to face forward. Breathe in, turning your head to the left, and then breathe out as your head returns to face forward again. This simple head turning is one of my all-time favourite breathing practices as it makes my head float and my consciousness instantly tunes into a more trance-like state.

- Choose a mantra to accompany each in-and-out breath, something linked to your lucid dreaming practice and your intent to become lucid in your dreams. For example, you might breathe in to the words: "I am..." and breathe out to "...lucid." Focus on these words and know they strengthen your chances of getting lucid. When you say these words in a lucid dream, they will cause the dream to stabilise and help you stay effortlessly lucid.

- Release the mantra when it feels a good moment to turn further inward and become very quiet and still. Observe your thoughts without getting sucked into their energy and stories.

- Now and again, you'll sense your thoughts quieten and you'll enter a wonderful, floaty, thought-free inner space. These are the golden moments of meditation, moments of pure awareness. Relax and allow these moments to expand. Adept meditators find that these moments lead to a state of great stillness and peace. With practice at building a relaxed, lucid mindset, these golden moments will naturally arise more often and last longer—just like dream lucidity. It's all connected.

- Thoughts will at some point begin again because this is the nature of the mind. Take this as a cue to remind you to pick up your lucid dreaming mantra again (or create a new one) and return your awareness to your breath. Meditate in this natural rhythm of mantra … peace … thoughts for as long as you like, without forcing yourself to do a certain amount of time. A short but regular practice is more valuable than one giant meditation session every three months, so pace yourself.

- You could also try a candle-gazing meditation—just be sure you don't fall asleep doing this and burn the house down. It's better to sit upright rather than lie down, to keep yourself awake, as it can be trance-inducing (or sleep-inducing!) to gaze at a flame. Light a candle and stare at the flame. Observe everything about it: the glowing core, the way it wavers in the air currents, its height and hunger, its aliveness. Focus. Notice the way the rest of your visual field goes dark, as if this flame is the only thing that exists. Repeat a lucid dreaming mantra: "I am lucid in my dreams." Throw in the occasional reality check: "Am I dreaming *now*? How do I know I'm awake?"

When we pay conscious attention to the here and now by meditating and focusing on our breath, we create greater clarity for a lucid mindset, and this enhances our ability to stay lucid in our dreams. If possible, meditate regularly, and make a lasting habit of noticing the thoughts that run through your mind during the day. This inner noticing is the core of mindfulness and it strengthens our capacity to be alert and lucid in our lives.

Music as a Path to Stable Lucid Dreams

When we mingle conscious awareness and unconscious imagery by day, we enhance our ability to stay lucid in our dreams. Music can help with this.

Music fills the air with vibrations that touch everything. When I beat my frame drum, the glasses in the kitchen cabinet vibrate. My body vibrates too, my blood sings, my feet dance to the beat. If I rest my fingers on our djembe drum while my little girl plays her saxophone, I feel the drumskin vibrate in response to her rich sound. When my husband joins in on his digital piano, bringing new sounds into the room, our bodies hum with the buzz that only music can create. I hasten to add that I'm really no musician—I love music and dancing, but I've never mastered an instrument nor have I had a single dance lesson in my life. But why would that stop me from leaping around having fun with drums and shakers and the like?

The way instruments and people vibrate together reminds me of the effect our thoughts, emotions, and intentions have on dreams. They vibrate into the heart of the dream and the dream vibrates right back. It's intimate and intense. When we emanate an optimal "vibration" in a lucid dream, in terms of mental clarity tinged with curiosity and cheerful openness, lucidity is easy. The dream is stable. There is no fear, no doubting voice, no mental confusion. We can explore without worrying about losing our awareness because we're vibrating at the right level to support lucid dreaming.

Explore different instruments and how they make you feel. We recently acquired a dome-like steel drum called a hand pan, and yes, one of its advantages (especially for kids) is that it looks like a spaceship, but it's also really melodious and can induce a relaxing, meditative state of mind. Other instruments I use in my yoga and meditation practice are Tibetan singing bowls. These have such a strong vibrating sound that a soft tap is enough to create a beautiful resonance that washes over you. Try closing your eyes to focus on the sound until it dies away. Identifying the exact millisecond when you can no longer hear the sound is another way of paying close attention to the present moment. Trance awareness can be enhanced and extended through music, and the following practices show how to link this to lucid dreaming.

⌇ *Practice 40* ⌇
Musical Trance

Music is a powerful ancient force that we can draw on (or tune in to!) to enhance lucid awareness and take us on imaginal journeys into the depths of our psyche.

- Choose your favourite chill-out music or pick up a recording of Tibetan singing bowls or shamanic drumming, then lie down comfortably and travel wherever you want to go. Allow your body to grow heavy, your limbs sinking into the bed while your mind remains alert.

- Enter the trance through the portal of music and imagine yourself flying lucidly over fantastic dreamscapes, or dancing to the beat at a lucid dream gathering.

- Revisit a dream that you love or allow fresh images to be created in this relaxed musical trance. Explore the feeling of lucidly navigating the imaginative spaces of your mind while the music fills your ears and vibrates throughout your body.

- Strongly intend and expect to have a similar lucid experience the next time you fall asleep. This musical trance can be really effective if you do it right before an afternoon nap and go directly into a wake-induced lucid dream (WILD).

⌇ *Practice 41* ⌇
Create an Earworm

Drum beats or just tapping out a rhythm on the tabletop can be great for creating a lucid dreaming mantra and fixing it in your mind. My lucid dream mantras always have a particular rhythm and some have a tune. Create your own "earworm" lucid dreaming mantra, one that feels catchy and fun to you. Hum it under your breath as you wait for your train (and do a reality check), use it in moments of peace and mental clarity, and connect it all the time with the strong expectation of using it successfully in a lucid dream to stay lucid for as long as you want.

Try a rhyme: "Strange though it may seem, I'm awake in my dream." Or something with repetitive elements that you can set to a well-known song:

"Am I dreaming now, dreaming now, dreaming now?" Sing it to yourself as you fall asleep—especially after a brief nighttime awakening. Remember to attach meaning to the words—this isn't an idle earworm, it has a purpose! If you imbue it with lucid intent, it could get you lucid and help you to *stay* lucid if your lucidity starts to fade.

⎨⎬ *Practice 42* ⎨⎬
Sing to Stay Lucid

There's one instrument we all possess, and we carry it with us everywhere we go: our voice. It doesn't matter if you're no Adele or Bieber, you can still sing in the shower, or while driving the car or cooking.

- Every time you sing, imagine you are lucid dreaming. Connect your singing firmly to the expectation of a highly stable lucid dream world.

- When you next get lucid, try singing in your dream. It's seriously magical to sing in a lucid dream. For a start, you can choose any voice you want. And secondly, no matter what your waking life voice sounds like, in a lucid dream your voice is a tool of power, a mighty force that can stop cows falling over crumbling dream cliffs, banish storm clouds, and cause the entire dream scene to tingle and vibrate with aliveness.

- Some lucid dreamers choose religious songs and find this can bring them sacred experiences such as floating in prayerful luminosity. Others borrow the voice of their favourite star and sing their lucid hearts out. Others experiment by creating different sounds with their dream voice box.

- Singing in a lucid dream focuses your awareness and mental clarity, as well as delivering a full-on energy rush. This raised consciousness stabilises the dream.

Become a Lucid Dream Yogi

Yoga, tai chi, Qigong, or any body-focused practice is great for building mental clarity and strengthening our ability to stay lucid in dreams. My twenty-five-year yoga practice has helped me develop body awareness (which helps me to notice when I'm in my dream body); mental focus and concentration;

a certain ability to stay calm in the face of crazy events; insights into the way the mind works; and balance—both mental and physical. I enjoy doing yoga in my lucid dreams as it's lovely to be effortlessly flexible and hold poses for as long as I like without tiring, as if I'm a top athlete or a bendy rubber woman. I can even levitate in my lucid dreams, and so can you! Yoga poses can also be helpful for staying lucid. One simple yoga pose that works wonders for me whenever I feel the dream becoming less stable is Mountain Pose. Here's my lucid dreaming version for you to test out:

⌒✺ *Practice 43* ✺⌒
Stable Mountain (Tadasana)

When we practise yoga in a dream, the results can be astonishing: mental clarity quickly increases and we feel calm and serene.

- Stand straight and tall in your dream body with your feet apart and your arms relaxed by your sides. You may find you grow several inches because the dream body is so flexible and responds to intentions, but don't let this distract you!

- Take a deep breath, imagining that you are breathing in CLARITY and LUCIDITY.

- Mentally "turn up the dimmer switch" so that your dream gets lighter and much clearer, the colours stronger. Notice the instant response of the dream. The buildings stop wobbling, the people stop dissolving. Everything becomes vibrant and conscious again.

- Breathe out any doubts about your ability to stay lucid, or any unhelpful thoughts.

- As you breathe in again, feel how grounded and focused you are in this dream. Feel the dream ground beneath your feet. Take in the dream scene with your eyes, allowing your lucid gaze to land in quick succession on different objects or images like a butterfly.

- Say aloud: "I'm lucid dreaming."

- Often one in-and-out breath is enough to stabilise the scene, but you may need a few more at first. Practise this technique during the day while vividly imagining it working the next time you stabilise a lucid dream.

Create your own simple grounding technique—whatever works for you and feels natural. You may choose to place your palms together over your chest in the prayer position, or raise both arms above your head in a sweeping circle. As long as you practise your technique by day and link it to a solid expectation of successful dream stabilisation, it should work for you.

Staying lucid in a dream can be a balancing act and it requires mental clarity and inner focus. Both things can be trained through balancing the physical body. There are several simple yoga poses we can practise to strengthen our mental clarity and inner focus. As a longtime yoga practitioner and instructor, I've found that when I take the extra step of linking this physical feeling of balance and mental focus to my lucid dreams, the effect is doubly strong. Yoga has plenty of balance poses, so there's a huge choice, but here are my two favourites:

᎒᎒ *Practice 44* ᎒᎒
Full Boat Pose (Paripurna Navasana)

Sit on the floor and hug your knees to your chest. Make sure there's nothing hard behind you in case you roll backwards. With a straight spine, tip yourself backwards just a little to bring your feet off the ground. Rock gently back into a position where you are perfectly balanced on your buttocks. For some, this may be surprisingly hard, but for others it's easy. Don't judge your ability, just see how it feels. Once you feel confident, play around by releasing your arms from around your knees and holding them straight out in front of you parallel to the floor, palms facing down. Extend your legs a little and see how it affects your balance.

For people who want this to be harder, try the full boat pose which involves keeping your legs together and stretching them straight up in the air with straight knees so that from the side your body forms a V shape. Balance with your arms out in front of you, or if you're feeling flexible, reach up and grip your toes with both hands. Never force any yoga pose! Respect your body's limits and be compassionate to your muscles and ligaments.

∽ *Practice 45* ∽
Tree Pose (Vrksasana)

Stand up straight and breathe. Focus your mind. Shift your body weight into your right foot. Raise your left foot and rotate your knee out to the left. Using your hand to help if need be, press the sole of that foot into your right leg at whatever height is comfortable. Breathing calmly, fix your gaze on a point at around eye level, and focus. Bring your palms together in the prayer position over your heart, or stretch your arms upwards like tree branches. Find your balance. If you wobble, notice this without getting flustered. If you have to put your foot down, so be it. Simply recover your feeling of calm focus and re-enter the pose.

If this pose is difficult for you, the simpler version is to keep the toes of your left foot on the ground, turn your knee outwards, and lean your heel against your right ankle. Always practise on both sides. This pose is so tightly linked to mental focus that your ability to stand stably in it could change a dozen times in one day. Observe how easy or hard it is at any given time and you'll find yourself able to assess your state of mind with precision. Visualise yourself standing steady and tall, bending slightly in the breeze like a tree.

Once you've attained balance in either of these poses, calmly repeat to yourself: "I am lucid. This is a dream. I easily stay lucid in this dream." As soon as you lose your balance, drop the mantra like a hot brick! Only use it when you are in perfect control of your balance and feel centred and focused. This is so you can quickly recreate the same feeling in a lucid dream as soon as you repeat this mantra.

Three More Lucidity Stabilisation Practices

You don't have to practise standing on one leg in order to stay lucid in a dream, so if yoga isn't your thing, here are some more stabilisation practices to suit every temperament.

∽ *Practice 46* ∽
Narrate Dream Events as They Unfold

Pick up the skills of a sports commentator and use them to narrate everything that's going on in your dream. This can be really funny to do and if lucidity is slipping, it's a fast way of pulling the dream back into clarity. Try it in combination with another stabilisation technique, such as rubbing your hands together vigorously. Mention the word "dream" often as you narrate what you see and experience so you don't forget you're dreaming. For example:

> "I see a purple-grey fishing boat on a vast lake, but now it's being pulled up into the air by some invisible force. It looks so surreal, and *woah*—I'm being pulled up too, into some kind of a vortex— *stay lucid, stay lucid*—now we've been set down on a mountain top and it's like a scene from *Heidi*, with spring flowers and dream cows chewing their cud with bells around their necks, except for this beached fishing boat reminding me this has to be a dream. When I touch the soil it's thick and peaty, as real as real could be, only this is a dream and the dream air is unbelievably clean and fresh, dream eagles soaring in a blue sky…"

Narrating the dream like this reminds you to stay present to everything you see, hear, touch, and experience. It grounds you within your dream world, even if you get swept up into a lucid vortex and deposited into a different dream. This is something that commonly happens when we lose our grip on one dream but manage to stay aware enough to be lucid in the next one when it materialises.

⟡ *Practice 47* ⟡
Pursue Your Lucid Dream Goal

Having a fixed goal of something we'd like to experience in a lucid dream can be a double-edged sword. As we saw in chapter 1, it can be brilliant to focus on a goal in order to encourage us to *get* lucid, but when beginner lucid dreamers go all-out to achieve a dream goal before learning how to stabilise and guide dreams, pursuing a goal too enthusiastically can result in losing lucidity.

On the other hand, when we feel lucidity slipping, it can be useful to sharpen our mental focus and intent by recalling a lucid dream goal. For a start, this distracts us from worrying about losing lucidity—when we worry about something, we're half expecting it to happen, and expectation in the lucid dream state is a force to be reckoned with.

It's good to combine your preferred stabilisation technique with the strong but calm intention to pursue your dream goal. You might look at your hands to calm down and focus, then look back at the scene, expecting it to stabilise. Once you see it working, announce your intention aloud: "In this lucid dream, I ride a white stallion through sunlit meadows." Sounds delightful—so go for it! When we practise active dream control, we seem less at risk of being sucked into the dream and losing lucidity, because of our keen sense of our "director" role. Try not to be perfectionist about your goal—if the white stallion fails to manifest but a large white dog appears, it's fine to ride that instead! Allow the dream its spontaneity and be ready to enjoy the joke.

ᕲᕳ *Practice 48* ᕲᕳ
Fly to Stabilise the Lucid Dream

Movement is a great way to solidify your presence in a lucid dream and stabilise the scene. Any physical activity can work well, from stroking a flower stem to taking large astronaut leaps. One utterly gorgeous experience is flying. This is a richly sensuous event that makes you feel completely alive, thrumming with energy, every pore of your skin tingling. It can also be an effective way of stabilising a lucid dream, as the strong sensations combine with your new bird's-eye perspective to activate your brain and sharpen your mental focus.

Once you're used to flying in your lucid dreams (chapter 7 has tips on successful dream flight), this becomes a lovely stabilisation technique to use when the dream starts to slip through your fingers and you begin to lose lucidity. Try flying low over the dream scene, focusing on every element and consciously expecting it to get clearer and clearer with each passing moment. Smile proudly to yourself when it does. You've got this!

In this chapter, we've explored how experimenting with creative lucid trances to simulate lucid dreaming trains us to become adept at balancing conscious awareness and unconscious imagery. We've looked at how lucid-dreaming-based meditation, mantras, yoga, and music can increase our mental clarity and focus. I've shared practices and techniques that train the mind to successfully stay lucid in dreams. After experimenting a little with each practice, you might like to choose your favourite three or four from this chapter and the previous one and work on honing them each time you become lucid in your dreams. The length of your lucid dreams should increase naturally as you become more adept at managing your mental focus and maintaining a high level of awareness.

When lucid awareness remains consistently high, there are no limits to what we can do in our lucid dreams! The next section explores the delightful art of guiding lucid dreams.

PART THREE:

Best Techniques for Guiding Lucid Dreams

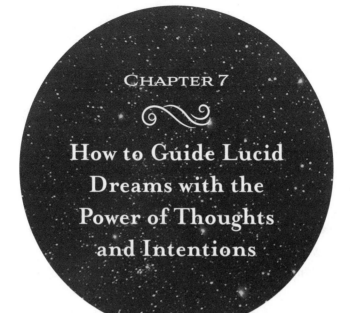

CHAPTER 7

How to Guide Lucid Dreams with the Power of Thoughts and Intentions

"I'm lucid in a dream and I've stabilised the scene. What do I do next?"

The exhilarating answer to this question is: "Why, anything you like!" It's true—in lucid dreams, we don't need to be held back by the laws of physics that govern our lives here on Earth. We can soar through the atmosphere powered by our intent, slow time down to a crawl, or even create a "dream freeze" by stopping time altogether in the dream. We can experience multiple dream realities simultaneously, go back in time, plunge into the future, die and die again, experience orgasmic ecstasy, turn invisible, and leap over rooftops without needing to catch our breath. We can shapeshift, becoming verdant moss, a python, an iridescent soap bubble. We can communicate wordlessly with dream figures and watch our thoughts impact the dream scene.

But we don't have to be time-bending, shapeshifting superheroes in our lucid dreams. We can sit peacefully on a dream hill smelling a yellow dream flower or talk with a wise friend. Our lucid dreaming consciousness can be drawn on for deep healing, spiritual communion, or philosophical musings. Or we can experiment like lucid scientists, testing the properties and laws of the dream world and creating hypotheses as to the ultimate nature of dream reality. In short, we can be ourselves and explore lucid dreaming in any way that appeals to us.

Of course, some may feel that's easier said than done. In my workshops, people ask me about "dream control." They want to know the rules—how to do it, why it doesn't always work, and the pros and cons. This section of the book aims to answer all these questions and provide a wealth of tips and solid practical techniques to help you develop and expand your ability to guide and shape your dreams. In this chapter, we'll start by looking at the different ways in which we can guide dreams.

Dreams Respond to Our Thoughts and Emotions

It's important to debunk the myth that just because we're lucid in a dream, we are controlling it. This simply isn't true. It's absolutely possible to be lucid and not actively guide events within the dream. For my PhD research into lucid dreaming as a creative tool, I identified four main levels of lucid dream engagement,[14] and two of these are passive, involving no attempt at dream control. I call the most passive form "passive observation," when we simply observe the film like a movie as it unfolds around us, keeping our thoughts quiet. The other passive form is "passive participation," when we go with the flow of whatever is happening in the dream when we become lucid, without purposefully changing things. A more active form is "sporadic control," when we occasionally nudge the dream in a particular direction or ask a question of the dream environment before waiting to see how the dream responds. I call the most active form "continuous control," when the dreamer keeps trying throughout the entire dream to guide and direct events. In terms of how active we are, there are many options for the lucid dreamer to choose from.

It must be said that dreams naturally and effortlessly respond to our emotions, expectations, doubts, and thoughts. This means that whether we're lucid or not, we can never 100 percent *not* influence a dream! We are the dream and it is us. We communicate with our dream through a sort of marvellously pure telepathy, no need for effortful words or gestures—we feel

---

14. Johnson, "The Role of Lucid Dreaming in the Process of Creative Writing."

something, and the dream knows and responds. We think something, and the dream knows and responds.

How does the dream respond? For a start, it may change the dream imagery and events to fit in with our expectations. For example, in a dream, a crystal chandelier falls from a high ceiling onto bare concrete. We stare in surprise—it hasn't shattered! It just sits there like a crystal-armed octopus. Weird. Yet the next time we glance over, there it is, lying in shards that have scattered realistically across the ground. The dream has reacted to our expectation that a "real life" crystal chandelier would shatter in this situation. It has sneakily corrected the visuals to fulfil our expectation! Expectation is a powerful force when we try our hand at guiding dreams.

Dreams are also adept at exaggerating details in response to our feelings. Our emotions and feelings have an instantaneous effect on dream happenings and dream imagery. Have you ever been in a dream and had a nervous thought about what might happen next, only to have it happen exactly as you feared? Perhaps you thought something like, "Oh no, I bet there are poisonous snakes in this jungle." Then lo and behold, what did you see but a poisonous snake slithering into your path? Dreams love to respond! They love to fulfil our expectations and our desire for drama.

A golden rule when guiding dreams is therefore: *pay attention to your thoughts and feelings!* Be ready to turn them around on a pin if you don't want them to manifest instantly. Lucid dreaming is the best mindfulness practice ever. The strange beauty of waking up in a dream gives us a rich consciousness jolt. We get to experience the impact of our thoughts, expectations, intentions, and emotions on our surroundings. We get to witness the astounding moment-by-moment creativity of our dreaming mind as it instantly translates all this input from us into streams of emotive dream imagery.

Before we dive into the "how" of dream control, let's look at our personal assumptions and beliefs about reality, because these have a lot of power in the lucid dream state.

What Do You Believe?

When we experiment with guiding dreams, it can be useful to check in with ourselves regarding our basic beliefs and assumptions about life, dreams, the cosmos, and how it all works. In the lucid dream state we may think we're prepared to turn our assumptions on their head, but in fact it can be harder than we anticipated to release cherished world views—even while we're dreaming! Some of our beliefs—even those about how the physical universe works—can trip us up on the path to exploring and guiding dreams. We can avoid some obstacles by checking in with ourselves about our personal belief system, as in the following practice.

⊙∾ *Practice 49* ∾⊙
Test Your Belief System

Try answering these questions to work out your stance towards dreaming and waking life.

1. Do you think it will be easy to guide dreams with your thoughts? Do you anticipate a steep learning curve? Or perhaps you fear this is something only gifted lucid dreamers can do? Write a sentence beginning: "Guiding my lucid dreams will be..."

2. In waking life, do you believe that our intentions, beliefs, thoughts, and desires have an impact on the physical universe?

3. Do you believe that we humans have attained the full extent of our knowledge about the laws of physics, and that all our conclusions are correct?

4. Do you believe dreams are solely produced by our brains, or do you think dreams are vaster than the brain and have a different source?

5. Who are you when you dream? It could be beneficial to make a few notes on this and return in a few months to see if anything has changed. Try writing responses to the following, without deliberating too much: How do you behave in your dreams? How do you feel in your dreams? Are you fearful, bold, sad, a pleasure-seeker? Do you explore your dream world with childlike curiosity, or do you get into highly emotional arguments and physical fights? Do you ever cry in your dreams?

6. Are you kind and respectful to dream people, or do you see them as figments of your imagination that you can do anything you like with?

7. Are you a different person in your dreams than you are in waking life? How so?

8. Do you think it's possible to change your dreaming self for the better? And how about your waking self?

9. Is there any overlap between dreaming and waking experience, or are these two separate states?

10. What do you believe will happen if you die in a lucid dream?

Your answers may come in handy as you set out to guide your dreams—especially if you find it hard to "make stuff happen" in a lucid dream, or if you have trouble getting off the ground when you try to fly in your lucid dreams. Be aware of any limiting assumptions you may have about the nature of reality, as these may hamper your open-mindedness (and therefore your ability to guide events) in the dream state. Take careful note of your answer to question #1: if you wrote "guiding my dreams will be hard," modifying this sentence to something more hopeful should ease your path somewhat.

Lucid dream exploration is a journey that can cause us to question some of our basic beliefs about physics, science, and the way we interact with the universe. It can cause us to question ourselves; who we are, how we handle relationships, and our attitude to life. This questioning can be the first step towards positive change. It's good to question things and stay curious, with a spirit of discovery. It's good to develop as a person, both in the dream world and the waking world, and since the two are inextricably interconnected, change in one world will automatically cause change in the other. It's also good to move briskly past mental blocks and preconceptions so that we encounter our lucid dream world with a fresh, open mind and a fearless heart.

What Are the Pros and Cons of Dream Control?

Even though lucid dreaming doesn't have to involve any active guiding of the dream, and even though no dreamer (lucid or non-lucid) can *avoid* interacting with the dream because it's naturally responsive to our thoughts, emotions, and intentions, I often hear objections to lucid dream control. Some people revolt against the idea of controlling or manipulating dreams as they feel that important psychological messages could be missed. What if a dreamer becomes lucid in a dream of a four-headed dragon and decides to fly away from it at the speed of light to have some fabulous dream sex instead? Wouldn't that poor dreamer miss out on what might have been a terrifying yet psychologically valuable encounter with a fire-breathing dragon?

Well, the nature of dreaming is such that nightmares are known to recur again and again until their message is received and understood by the dreamer. That four-headed dragon will likely return in a different guise until we face it with courage or unpack its message through waking dreamwork. This is one reason why it can be so valuable to become lucid in nightmares, in order to face our own shadow side and heal. (More on how to do that in chapter 8.)

Also, most people do not spend the majority of their night of sleep dreaming lucidly—they may have one or two lucid dreams, then none for a few days, then another one, and so on. This means there is still absolutely loads of non-lucid-dreaming time where we can receive any psychological messages or guidance that we need. But let's not forget that lucid dreaming can be just as valuable in terms of deep psychological insights and self-understanding as non-lucid dreaming can. In a lucid dream, our conscious awareness enables us to experience startling insights and act in profoundly healing ways, as discussed in chapters 8 and 9.

The other point is that no matter how much we enthusiastically try to direct and control a lucid dream, there will always be elements beyond our control, or elements that we didn't consciously "create." The shape of the spaceship, the colour of a dream person's coat, the music that drifts in from somewhere... who invented those? Our dreaming mind is an instant world-creator, and in the dream world there is always, always room for spontaneity.

I'm a firm believer that any kind of dream fun is profoundly *good for us*. Have you ever woken up laughing out loud at something wonderfully funny that happened in your dream? Or have you woken up blissed-out from a flying dream? Or smiling from your heart because in your dream you met a precious friend? Or have you awoken savouring the ecstatic sexual encounter you just dreamed? And how does waking up this happy affect your daytime mood? It improves it! Beyond any doubt. When we wake up happy, we have more of the strength and humour we need to tackle problems and dilemmas.

Dream fun is not to be sniffed at. It can be as psychologically powerful as being gobbled up by a four-headed dream dragon!

Following many years of experimentation, my stance on dream control is that it can be fascinating to go with the flow of a dream when we become aware that we're dreaming. It can also be incredible to consciously direct the action towards a particular experience, ask questions of the dream, or purposefully draw on the lucid dream state for healing. We act in our waking lives all the time, right? We decide to drop karate lessons and take up rowing instead, we decide to phone an old friend, or we take a trip to Indonesia. Why not act in our lucid dreams if it feels right?

As in waking life though, it's helpful to remain receptive and responsive and not force things. Lucid dreaming is a conversation with the deepest part of ourselves, and if we are too rigid, we risk supressing the natural spontaneous creative expression of the dream. This is illustrated by the following lucid dream shared with me by Bob Hoss, co-editor of *Dreams That Change Our Lives* and director of the IASD dream conferences:

> I was attempting to impose my very specific desires on the dream. I found myself frustrated, all alone in a pretty dull dream. At that point the lucid dream itself personified as a woman—"the secretary." I asked her, "Who are you?" She said, "I am the secretary." I asked, "What are you here for?" She said, "I am here to take orders from you, but I can't really do much creatively if that's all you want me to do."

The dream secretary's words sum it up: when we determinedly impose our control on a lucid dream, we may cramp some of its marvellous creativity. I've found that when I engage respectfully with dream people and animals and do not force my agenda too rigidly, it can be a wonderful and highly creative journey of discovery to guide a dream. The beauty of lucid dreaming is that each person can experiment and decide for themselves their own preferred way of engaging with their lucid dreams.

Why Is Lucid Dream Sex Sometimes so Difficult?

It's always interesting to see how the dream responds when we attempt to guide events and carry out specific dream goals. It's only through experimenting that we'll be able to work out the rules of the game and maintain our lucid focus no matter what happens (and dreams are full of surprises). One popular area of dream guiding that people write to me about is sex. Dreamers feel frustrated when the dream sex they were so intent on having doesn't materialise in the way they wanted. There are reports of vibrant sex goddesses melting into puddles, turning into zoo animals, or reacting lifelessly, with a lolling head and hideous blank eyes. That's enough to turn anyone off!

But there are ways to get a dream back on track; it just takes mental focus and a familiarity with the practices in the getting and staying lucid parts of this book. Here's an excerpt from a dream of David Jay Brown's in his book *Dreaming Wide Awake*, where we see the various obstacles that come along to thwart him as he pursues his goal of having dream sex.

> I found a willing partner but had some trouble getting all of her clothing down past her butt. She was on all fours, sticking her butt out and wiggling it, but there were so many layers of clothing to pull down—four or five layers of pants, pantyhose, underwear. I finally got them all down, got an erection, and entered her […] I was really enjoying the delightful sensations, knowing that my time there was limited, and I was trying to see if I could actually orgasm in the dream. However, before I could come, the woman turned into a rubber doll. Actually, she became just a partial, life-size doll's body, just the backside and butt, made out of rubber or latex, and she was hollow, there was no front to her, I realized with a sudden shock that I was just having sex with this rubber thing.[15]

Obstacles pop up regularly in this dream: the many layers of clothing; the woman's transformation into a rubber doll; and as the dream continues, all passion dies. There are various points at which the dreamer might have taken a moment to stabilise the dream and gain more lucid focus, which would

---

15. Brown, *Dreaming Wide Awake*, 341–2.

have probably stabilised the image of the dream woman. Simply saying with power and conviction "I am lucid" can snap the dream into clarity. Difficulty guiding dreams or carrying out dream goals is often a lucidity issue rather than a dream guiding issue. It can also happen when we haven't yet refined our powers of expectation and intent to the point where they automatically manifest to keep us on track.

∽ *Practice 50* ∽
A Guide to Successful Lucid Dream Sex

When we take time to prepare the ground for a lucid sex dream, it's much more likely to manifest just as we desire.

- Spend time fantasising about exactly what you'd like to do in your ideal erotic lucid dream. Think about it in the shower, or while drifting off to sleep. The really important thing is to feel supremely confident that this scenario can and will happen easily when you are lucid in a dream. If you like, sketch your erotic scenario, or write it out in sizzling detail to solidify the powerful tools of expectation and intent. Who knows, you may even discover a new talent as an erotic fiction writer!

- When you become lucid, use the CLEAR lucid dream stabilisation technique from chapter 5. Once the dream is stable, try this trick to help a gorgeous, willing sexual partner to appear: stand still, building your intent with a deep, steady breath, then declare: "When I turn around, I will find a gorgeous partner who is longing to have sex with me." Then turn around deliberately, fully expecting to behold your lucid dream lover.

- Another way to make the ideal partner appear is to use a power word or gesture of your own invention. If you plan to do this, be sure to weave that word or gesture firmly into your waking fantasies so that it has an instant effect in the lucid dream state.

- In a dream, there's no need for a conventional sexual partner in order to reach orgasm. Psychologist Dr. Patricia Garfield, author of the lucid dreaming classic, *Creative Dreaming*, reports exploding into orgasm simply by plummeting from the sky into the ocean, or using objects ranging from a rosebud to a water fountain to pleasure herself in lucid dreams. So, if your desired partner never shows up, or disintegrates in the heat of passion, there are always other options.

- It can be rewarding to appreciate lucid dream lovers as part of the magical creativity of lucid dreaming and treat them respectfully. You never know, this may have lasting positive repercussions on the kind of lucid dream sex you experience … not to mention the kind of waking life sex you attract.

- Once you embark on your sexual encounter, don't let the excitement make you lose your lucid focus—be ready to revert to one of the CLEAR steps any time you feel less aware.

I Can't Seem to Fly in My Lucid Dreams! What's Happening?

Flying seems to be another lucid dream act that some people lament is way harder than they thought. Yet lucid dream flying can be so gloriously easy! It's all about stable lucidity plus our expectations and beliefs about what is or is not possible. In the following dream I became lucid in a huge, light building:

> I feel myself float higher and decide to explore the ceiling. It's so high! I shoot up a wall and backflip at the top, then fly around close to the roof. Such bliss! There's nothing like this sensation— light and free. I twist and turn and play …

The playfulness of dream flying is not to be underestimated—when we get too earnest about lucid dream goals, we risk thwarting them. It's good to feel light, happy, and confident in a lucid dream, because the dream picks up on this and anything is possible. Relaxing and enjoying ourselves leads to a stress-free engagement with the dream scene, and if at this point we want to guide events, it's much easier than if we're feeling pressured or stressed about it. Since some beginner lucid dreamers have trouble achieving liftoff, here are some tips for an easy lucid dream flight.

⟨∽ *Practice 51* ∽⟩
A Guide to Flying in Lucid Dreams

Once you're adept at stabilising a lucid dream, flying shouldn't pose a problem, especially if you integrate some of the following tricks and tips.

- *Expect* flying to be easy! This is vital. Visualise successful dream flights before you go to sleep at night.

- Remind yourself that gravity has no real meaning in a lucid dream—it only exists if we believe it does. In dreams, flying is a normal mode of transport, like walking or taking the bus.

- In the dream, jump into the air and spread your arms wide, willing yourself to soar upwards. The truth is, the arm position is irrelevant, but some people find that involving the arms helps them to get off the ground. Others find that adopting a Superman-style stance with both arms straight out helps. Discover what works for you. If you can't get airborne, imagine yourself turning into a soap bubble and floating upwards, or having a motorised backpack that can jet you into the sky at the push of a button. Be inventive and believe in your own invention. It's absolutely possible to "trick" yourself in this way so that suddenly you find yourself flying.

- If you can only fly sluggishly, this is a sign that you need to raise your lucid awareness and stabilise the dream using the CLEAR stabilisation technique or another of your choice.

- Keep trying *without getting frustrated or feeling defeated* until flying simply happens. Banish any doubtful thoughts—these will seriously hamper you if you give them power. Replace them quickly with the positive expectation of an easy liftoff. Smile, laugh, relax. Allow your leaps to be gazelle-like, lifting you up into the air. Then simply soar along from there.

- Some people report vertigo when they find themselves high above the ground. Take a calming breath and remind yourself in a lighthearted way that this is a dream and the high-up visual perspective is a dream creation. You are not in any danger! Try a mantra: "I can fall from the sky and not die … I am free as a bird up high." You also have the option of flying lower: strongly intend to fly six feet above the ground, point your arms if this helps to direct you, and skim down to your preferred height.

- Let your breath be your engine when ascending and descending. Breathe in and imagine that you are a bright balloon and the dream air is helium. Feel yourself rising higher with every in-breath as your lungs inflate. It's so easy! The thrill of leaving the ground makes you feel even lighter and you are able to deftly weave a flight path wherever you want to go. To return to the ground, purse your mouth into an "O" shape and imagine that each long exhalation sends you gently down to earth.

- Enjoy yourself. This is seriously one of the most gloriously cool experiences in the world. Swoop over your dreamscape, blow a kiss to any people or animals you see, visit the stars, or fly straight into the golden fireball of the sun. You can't get hurt. You will wake up safely in your bed, so be free!

The People and Images We Meet in Our Dreams

A "dream figure" doesn't have to be a person or an animal. It can be any part of the dream that we sense has a particular presence and reality to it. It can be a creature we've never seen before, a waterfall, or a star. Just as in fantasy fiction, in lucid dreams animals can talk and wise beings take on the guise of towering columns of blue light or mysteriously glowing bushes (as I've found in my own dreams). And these high-consciousness dream figures seem to *want* us to become lucid. Many lucid dreamers hear a "voice of God" booming from the sky. I had the following dream during an afternoon nap:

> I'm driving along when I see an astonishing sight: a pink double-decker bus, sideways on, rising into the air! Simultaneously I hear these words spoken very loudly: "YOU ARE DREAMING ALL OF THIS!"

How much more of a lucidity cue do we need than that? The whole dream conspires to help us to get lucid. For avid lucid dreamers, that really is a dream come true! When I explored lucid dreaming intensively in my twenties, I was often amazed by the insightful things dream people would say to me, or the way certain dream animals looked at me with a searing, super-lucid gaze that jolted me into higher lucidity. It interested me when dream people contradicted me or expressed opinions that I hadn't considered. It was as if some of them had a mind of their own, and I was fascinated.

Years later, my research led me to experiment. In lucid dreams I would summon the fictional characters I had invented as part of my first novel *Breathing in Colour*. This was to see if meeting my characters in the multi-sensory, super-realistic dimension of lucid dreaming would yield any fresh information about them or help my creative writing process.

In one lucid dream, I hung out with my artist character, Taos. It was exciting to be in his presence and see him fully embodied in my dream. He had an animal sensuality and was pretty moody. When I assured him that my main female character, Alida, would be all right, he turned and growled: "How do you know that? You may be the author, but you're not God!"

Well, that told me! I was taken aback that he seemed resentful of me (and yes, in all honesty, I had seen myself as his sole creator until then, so I probably deserved to be taken down a peg!). I was also surprised at how protective he was of Alida, who he barely knew at that early stage of the novel. Then I noticed he was holding his paintbrush in his left hand—and I'd thought he was right-handed! This final surprise woke me up with a jolt. I reflected on this lucid dream and suddenly understood that Taos was so defensive about Alida because she had already found her way into his heart. Aha! Now a new sub-plot for the novel opened up in my mind. I ran to my writing desk, slipped into the Lucid Writing trance, and wrote down what would happen next.

Does It Matter How We Treat Dream Figures?

Some of the most spine-tingling encounters I've had in lucid dreams involve animals. I've danced with elephants, lived in the jungle with a Bengal tiger, turned into a dolphin, discovered a baby bird napping on my bedside table, met the mother of all lizards in a luminous bardo zone, encountered a frozen stallion made of champagne, and had an ecstatic lucid kundalini awakening with a green serpent. Many of my dream animals are recurring figures in my dreams and they take on the role of guides, showing me when I need to pay attention to things in my life.

My dream tigers have a very strong presence in my dreams and are often linked to my creativity—I'm like a volcano if something stops me from writing or doing art. The inner tension builds and builds until I'm close to exploding. I'll dream a tiger comes right up to me and takes my arm in his jaw, forcing me to look at him. Or he'll come and stand right on my balcony, his massive head inches from mine. Or he'll corner me in the kitchen. These tigers force me to pay attention to my wild side and get creative ... or else! When I'm in my creative flow, my dream tigers lounge peacefully on river banks or let me stroke them. Dream animals can be the most valuable friends and allies. Look out for them in your lucid dreams and always give them the time of day—it's worth it!

In general, being respectful to dream figures yields huge rewards. I hear from lucid dreamers who say they treat dream people like cannon fodder, ripping them up with machine guns or beating them up or raping them. "They're figments of my imagination," they say, "they're like a computer game invented by me, so what does it matter?" But then some of them ask, "Why do I wake up feeling bad after doing this?"

I'm not here to judge how people want to act in their lucid dreams, and I feel everyone is capable of finding the way that makes them feel comfortable. I encourage people to test the assumptions they have about the dream world. ("It's all a figment of my imagination," or "It doesn't matter if I rape and murder in my dreams" are two assumptions that invite further reflection.) I suggest that people experiment with different ways of relating to their dreams to see how that makes them feel.

My own view is that on some level, we are responsible for our actions, whether they take place in the dream state or in the waking state. If we practise kindness in lucid dreams, being kind in waking life is easier too, and my own experience has taught me that on the deepest level, we are not separate from others: we are all one. So, it makes sense to be kind.

Some lucid dreamers decide they need advice on a particular problem and hassle a dream figure for answers in what would be perceived as a little rude or abrupt if it happened in waking life. Then they wonder why the dream figure gives them the brush-off. Experienced lucid dreamers find it can transform everything if, instead of leaping into things with our own agenda and making everything revolve around us, we pause to talk respectfully to dream people and are prepared to listen to whatever they have to say before asking them questions about our life issues. Also, an initial calm greeting or chat can also help us to see pretty quickly if this dream person is the best one to ask for advice.

Some dream figures simply aren't too bright; they can lack awareness and seem puppet-like. Others seem super-conscious—we get a little shock when we look into their eyes because they are so present and alert. These are the best ones to go to with our questions. This next practice shows the four main levels of awareness of dream figures that I've come up with. There will be other levels for sure, and every dreamer is different, so you may like to customise these "types" as you explore more deeply.

⚭ *Practice 52* ⚭
How Conscious Are Your Dream Figures?

Would you wander out onto the high street and ask a random stranger "Where is my life going?" or "Should I split up with my girlfriend?" True— for some, this sort of exchange can and does happen after pub closing time, but don't we at least look people in the eye and exchange a few words first? In lucid dreams there's sometimes the sense that we'll wake up imminently, so we stress out, trying to squeeze in our goal. But when we become adept at stabilising the dream, we can chill out more.

This guide is to help you to find the best dream person to spill out your heart to, while remembering one vital thing about lucid dreaming: since the lucid dream itself hums with awareness, directing a question *to the dream itself* can be just as beneficial, if not more so, than seeking out a dream figure to ask. In many cases, the dream figure can be seen as a kind of prop—we're used to talking to people in waking life, so we feel the need to find an image of a person to talk to in a lucid dream, to make it seem real for us. But we could just as easily direct our question to the underlying, thrumming awareness that lucid dream imagery emerges from.

- *Zombies:* These are the "film extras" of lucid dreaming. They have little more substance than a cardboard cutout and are non-responsive if you try to talk to them. The more lucid we are, the fewer zombies we meet.

- *Puppets:* These are rather cute in their own way. They'll talk to you, but you'll have the distinct impression that you're the one putting words into their mouths by expecting a particular response, or by telepathically supplying them with the words. If you imagine them laughing, then guess what? They laugh! Puppets do their best to keep up socially and maintain the illusion that they think their own thoughts, but their act is pretty easy to see through.

- *Conscious equals:* Some dream figures seem able to talk to us on an equal level. They don't seem to intuit our thoughts and spit them right back out at us like the puppets do; instead they respond with insight. They can surprise us and they can argue coherently. Often, they take on the role of guides or mentors and can be helpful at initiating us further into the mysteries of lucid dreaming.

- *Super-aware:* You'll know if you meet one of these. Super-aware dream figures seem even more conscious than we are! They seem to act autonomously and possess a higher awareness and deep knowledge. It is electrifying (and occasionally terrifying) to find ourselves in the presence of these super-aware figures who often manifest in non-human form, such as a glowing globe of light. Keeping our cool and not giving in to fear can make or break this type of encounter. When we stay calm and curious, we can learn so much from this type of lucid dream figure. If things get too scary, you can always wake yourself up—but it can be immensely rewarding to hold onto your courage and stay in the dream.

- Whenever you ask lucid dream figures a question about your life situation, your future, the nature of reality, or any other pressing question you may have ("What are next week's lottery numbers?" "Will

I get laid this weekend?"), be alert for nonsensical or insanely cryptic responses, but it's best never to dismiss anything in the dream, as sometimes we only understand the message (if there is one) once we've woken up.

- No matter who we ask, remember that just asking aloud—*asking the dream itself*—is really effective, because the lucid dream is conscious. Responses may manifest through a voice booming out from nowhere, or a stream of imagery showing us a particular sequence of events, or the appearance of a person or image. We might suddenly be awash with a strong emotion or experience a flood of insight.

    When we ask profound questions in a lucid dream, such as "What happens after we die?" or "What is the meaning of life?" what often happens is that we get swept up by an invisible wind and transported at top speed into a vast sparkling lucid void, or we are pulled downward into a spiralling black hole. Don't be afraid if this happens! Just hold on to your hat and go with that wind, because this sort of response from the lucid dream often ends in incredibly blissful states where we receive knowledge and experience pure interconnected oneness. (More on that exciting state of affairs in chapter 9.)

Make New Dream Friends

If we barge through our lucid dreams with the attitude that dream figures are there to serve us and that we are the king in this dream and can do whatever the hell we like, we are bound to run into trouble along our lucid dreaming path. At some point we may develop a "block" around an aspect of lucid dreaming and not know why, or we may stay stuck forever in the playground zone of lucid dreaming and never glimpse the absolute amazingness of deep lucid dreaming.

But when we are willing to learn from our lucid dream figures and interact with them respectfully, everything changes. We'll make new friends! Our lucid dream friends (who may take on different guises in each new dream) can and will open doors for us, as well as doing everything in their power to get us lucid. If you experience a lucidity boost in a dream, the dream will overall become more conscious along with you. You are the lucid dream, and the lucid dream is you.

⊙✺ *Practice 53* ✺⊙
How to Interact with Dream Figures
so They Support Our Lucidity

When we enlist the help of dream figures to get us lucid, we may quickly unleash a flurry of lucid dreams as they respond by dropping hints to us that "this is a dream" or invent other ways to raise our lucidity levels.

- As a basic fact of your lucid dreaming practice, be open to the fact that *any* dream person, animal, object, or landscape you encounter in a lucid dream (or any dream, for that matter) may have something valuable to teach you. Yes, even a dream slug or a zombie dream person. You never know! In dreams, pretty much everything is imbued with emotional meaning. Landscapes, dream figures, and even our own dream selves can all transform in the blink of an eye, so stay alert for changes.

- Cultivate an attitude of respect, compassion, and generosity with dream figures, and they will open new doors for you and help you in surprising ways.

- Offer the dream figure a gift, especially if they're being aggressive towards you or barring your way. Just put your hand in your pocket while fully expecting the perfect gift for them to emerge. Offer it with love in your heart. Even if the gift turns out to be nothing more than a raggedy bit of tissue you found in the depths of your pocket, or a half-eaten toffee, the act of offering it with love often transforms the dream person or animal swiftly into a BFF. Just don't assume the same trick will work in waking life (unless you keep one pocket stocked with diamonds and the other with doggie treats).

- When we interact consciously and compassionately with our dream figures, they awaken along with us. They become highly conscious and eager to help us to get lucid, stay lucid, and discover all manner of wise and wonderful things in the dream world.

———

In this chapter, we've investigated how to guide lucid dreams with the power of thoughts and intentions. We've considered our basic beliefs and assumptions about the universe. We've examined the pros and cons of dream control, and we've looked at the value of interacting respectfully with the people we meet in lucid dreams. We've seen that every part of the lucid dream environment is alive and conscious to differing degrees. I've shared practical guides to having successful lucid dream sex and superb flying dreams.

Now it's time to move into the "worst-case scenario": nightmares! We'll see how lucidity can help us reach powerful, healing transformations when we're faced with frightening dreams.

Chapter 8

Facing and Embracing Nightmares

When we are lucid in a dream, we can see how swiftly our thoughts, emotions, and expectations cause the dream reality to change. When we grow fearful ("Oh jeez—what if that shadowy guy in the corner pulls out a knife?"), then what do you suppose will happen nine times out of ten in the dream? Yes—the shadowy guy brandishes a gleaming knife. Our fear intensifies still further with the panicked thought: "He's going to kill me!" As we stand rooted in terror, fully expecting to meet a terrible end, what happens? The man springs towards us, wielding his knife.

Well, this dream could end badly, right? But what happens if, at this moment in the dream, we experience a thunderbolt of insight?

If at this point in the dream we realise that *we are dreaming this*, that *we are safely asleep in our bed*, and that *the terror we are feeling is self-created*, our fear may vanish in the blink of an eye (or the flash of a knife). Calm and lucidly aware, we face our would-be attacker with curiosity.

"Who are you and what do you want?" we enquire kindly.

This radical shift in our attitude changes everything about the dream. The scene grows lighter, the knife is clearly a fake one. We look into the attacker's face and in wonder we see our own face looking back at us.

"Wait—you're *me*?" we ask.

In answer, we receive an embarrassed shrug and a nod, along with the mumbled reply: "I just feel like you've been ignoring me."

Touched, we open our arms and hug this neglected part of ourselves. Instantly, there is an incredible expansion in our heart, a sense of overwhelming love, mingled with a kind of giddy relief, like a homecoming.

When we are able to respond to scary dream figures with love instead of fear, we can transform not only the dream itself, but ourselves. It may sound simplistic, or corny. But it's true. People usually wake up from this kind of integrative lucid dream buzzing with happiness or with a sense of deep content. Lucidity can act as a trigger for us to change the way we habitually react, but even if we don't become lucid in a dream, we find that the more waking dreamwork we do, the more this kind of outcome will spontaneously arise in our non-lucid dreams, too. When we are aware of the possibilities, our unconscious mind internalises them too and will use them. In this way, over time we become more resourceful dreamers and happier people.

Nightmares are dreams that have such upsetting or stressful content that they usually wake us up. Bad dreams and nightmares commonly occur, even in adults. This chapter looks at ways of reacting with lucidity to nightmares, either during the actual dream, or after we wake up from it. When we ignore or supress our nightmares, they tend to recur until we receive their message, so becoming lucid in a recurring nightmare is a good thing as it can enable us to understand and act on its message. We'll also look at sleep paralysis and how to free ourselves from fear in that state so we can move directly into a beautiful lucid dream.

In many ways, this chapter is all about fear. Let's cut to the chase and look at a fearful question that a surprising amount of people have about lucid dreaming.

"Could I physically die during a lucid dream?"

A lucid dream is simply a dream in which you are aware that you are dreaming. Lucid dreaming takes place in normal stages of sleep that we all move through every night of our lives. It's no more dangerous than non-lucid dreaming. There's no evidence that people have died while lucid dreaming, but if anyone did, how would we know? Secretly, I've always felt that dying in my sleep would be my preferred way to go, one day when I'm old; it sounds blissful, like floating into the light. Anyone could die at any stage of waking or sleep. However, after many thousands of adventurous lucid dreams, I have always woken up safely in my bed. So have other lucid dreamers.

Sometimes I think there's too much mystical thinking about lucid dreaming because people write to me seeming to seriously believe that if they die in a lucid dream, they will actually, physically die. This idea instils in them a terror of their spontaneous lucid dreams. It seems such a pity, such a waste of potentially remarkable and healing lucid dream experiences to view them this way. It seems to me it's never worth being dominated by our fears. On the contrary, why not walk towards our fears? It's the first step to understanding them. Lucid dreaming enables us to hold our heads high and walk towards our fears.

Dreams are rich with symbolism, and death in any dream, lucid or non-lucid, can be symbolic of transformation. Dying in a dream might represent finishing with one phase or stage of life and preparing for the next, or it might represent an "ego-death" as we throw off a more self-centred approach to life and grow spiritually. Some people choose to "die" in a lucid dream in order to face their fears about death and come closer to understanding what happens at the end of life. One lucid dreamer I know allowed himself to be torn apart by a dinosaur. Another plunged off a towering dream cliff. Another flew into the molten core of the sun. They all woke up safely in their beds.

When we are able to remind ourselves that "After any lucid dream, I wake up safely in my bed!" we set ourselves free. We liberate ourselves so we are able to engage fearlessly with our nightmares. We can relax in the knowledge that even when things get terrifying in the dream world, we are safe. Armed with this knowledge, we can walk bravely to meet our nightmares.

Why Change a Nightmare?

Changing the ending of a nightmare can be powerfully therapeutic and has even been successfully used by people who experience recurring, horrific nightmares due to post-traumatic stress disorder (PTSD). Imagine a veteran whose buddy was shot in the head right in front of him in the war. Now, in recurring nightmares, he relives the tragic scene and feels overcome with anguish and powerlessness. How can changing the dream story possibly help?

Because we're working with imagery, we can reimagine the scene and change this imagery. For example, instead of the soldier shooting the veteran's friend in the head, he lays down his gun and admits that war is a terrible thing. The remarkable thing is that *even if in real life the veteran saw his friend getting shot in the head*, on the unconscious level of his nightmares this simple act of changing the imagery has made a difference. A new path has been forged; new imagery overlays the old. If the veteran then focuses on his new, changed dream by writing it down and re-reading it each day, this reinforces the new story, and the recurring nightmares may well reduce in frequency and intensity, or even stop altogether. This technique is called Imagery Rehearsal Therapy.

I just gave an example of one of the hardest cases: a trauma-induced recurring nightmare. But changing the imagery of a nightmare can have therapeutic benefits on any level—it can help us with a stressful "I'm not ready!" dream about an upcoming public speaking event (we find ourselves naked on stage), or a "disaster" dream about our imminent house move (the removal van rolls into a lake). When I first started teaching my Lucid Writing method, I taught it as a creativity technique, but as people started spontaneously resolving nightmares in my workshops, I understood its full potential as a tool for healing. The next practice shows how a few short minutes of Lucid Writing can help us unwrap the meaning of a disturbing dream or a nightmare, or resolve it in healing ways.

∽ *Practice 54* ∽
Changing a Nightmare with Lucid Writing

Have you ever wished you could have become lucid in a nightmare? You can add lucidity to the dream once you awaken from it. Changing and reimagining dream images is a simple yet powerful process. One lady had a nightmare about a huge, vibrating demon. In her Lucid Writing, it turned spontaneously into a giant golden Buddha and then disappeared. She said afterwards that this had changed the energy of the nightmare, and that the terror had simply gone.

Another woman dreamed of a wild, crashing river. In her Lucid Writing it morphed into a calm sea and she realised that rivers flow into the sea; they are one. This triggered the realisation that she had been frightened her whole life of being swept along by her mother like a wild river, but she didn't have to be scared of losing herself. She felt this insight gave her an answer to a stuck part of herself that she'd been struggling with for many years. She now felt free to go with the flow of life and trust that everything would work out well.[16]

- Enter a lucid trance by closing your eyes, taking deep breaths and using the golden light visualisation from Practice 38. Imagine light cascading over your body. Then bring your nightmare into your mind's eye, knowing that if things get upsetting, you can stop this process any time by opening your eyes.

- When your nightmare is vivid in your mind, notice the key images and emotions. Release any fear or anxiety, knowing that you are awake and safe. Allow the nightmare imagery to move and transform, let the dream story change before your eyes.

- Take a pen and write without stopping, describing what you see and writing without any agenda, allowing associations and ideas to flow freely.

- Be open to receiving knowledge from your nightmare, and be open to healing resolution, but it's not wise to force anything to happen. Lucid Writing is more like watching and listening to a spontaneous flow of inner imagery and inner wisdom than actively creating. However, you might feel inspired to ask a question of one of the elements in your nightmare, just as you might if this were a lucid dream: "Do you have a message for me?" "Why are you giving me such a mean stare?" "What do those massive tentacles of yours represent?" Or, "How does it feel to be you?" Simply write down any response you receive without

---

16. Johnson, *Llewellyn's Complete Book of Lucid Dreaming*, 145.

judging it and allow the imagery to keep flowing. Critical judgement is not useful in this process—just write, and keep writing until you are done.

- Re-read your Lucid Writing and underline anything that speaks to you or feels important. If you feel there's something you still need to understand about your nightmare, you can always take one element of your writing or a core image from your nightmare and use that as a starting point to "write without stopping" again.

- Adapt this technique to suit you. Not everyone enjoys writing, so you could try Lucid Doodling—working solely with images—or Lucid Talking—simply talking into a recording device while resting with your eyes closed and watching your nightmare imagery transform in your mind's eye.

Nightmare Solutions

One of the core nightmare resolution techniques I've developed is similar to Lucid Writing in terms of the internal transformation of dream imagery, but it's designed to be used immediately after waking up from a nightmare when we are still super close to the creative state of dreaming. It's called the Lucid Imaging Nightmare Solution. Lucid Imaging is like lucid dreaming awake. It's like Lucid Writing without the pen, observing and guiding dream imagery in our mind's eye, so it happens very naturally when we're in the middle of a night of sleep.

Please be aware that this technique is not recommended for those suffering from anxiety, depression, psychosis, or personality disorder, or people who have recently experienced trauma or bereavement. Some nightmares should not be worked on alone as they can involve intensely emotional and deep-rooted issues. Instead, find a trained therapist to help you with any underlying issues.

For many people who do not suffer from the above listed issues but who have trouble getting back to sleep after a nightmare, this technique is ideal. It gives you a calm space in which to interact lucidly and constructively with unsettling dream imagery and achieve a certain measure of resolution before slipping back to sleep and perhaps even moving directly into a wonderful lucid dream. As with any other technique, see what works for you and adapt it to suit your needs.

⊖∞ *Practice 55* ∞⊖
The Lucid Imaging Nightmare Solution (LINS)[17]

1. Attend to Your Body

As soon as you wake up from a nightmare, do whatever you need to calm yourself and make yourself comfortable. Some nightmares result in hefty physical reactions, like a wildly beating heart or sweat-drenched pyjamas. Drink water if you need to, and take deep, calming breaths. Then lie comfortably, close your eyes, and breathe calmly. Ask yourself if you want to work with this nightmare now or not. If the answer is yes, remind yourself that you are relaxing safely in your bed and can stop the process whenever you want to, simply by opening your eyes and sitting up.

2. Re-enter Your Nightmare

Recall the dream imagery as far back as you can. What were you doing before the dream grew unpleasant? Knowing that you are now safe in your bed, allow the imagery to resurface in your mind's eye. If you have difficulty summoning mental imagery, you can use the storyline of your nightmare as a way in. Notice any associations you have with the dream images and events, but don't agonise or obsess about possible meanings. If at any point in this process you feel very frightened, upset, or unsafe, stop immediately. Some nightmares are simply too strong and disturbing to face alone.

3. Identify the "Tipping Point"

Pinpoint the moment when feelings such as fear, guilt, or anxiety grew strong, or when the monster reared its ugly head. This moment is like the tipping point on a pair of scales. It is the moment that your dream turned into a nightmare. Your task now is to restore the balance. Decide where in the dream action you want to begin to change events or your attitude towards them. Beginning just before the tipping point usually works well.

---

17. This material previously appeared in *Llewellyn's Complete Book of Lucid Dreaming*.

4. Imagine This Is a Lucid Dream

Rerun the script to resolve the dream crisis. Watch the imagery as it unfolds and reacts responsively to your thoughts, questions, needs, and guidance. This is a highly creative state of consciousness because the mind is alert yet your body is relaxed and close to sleep. In lucid imaging, you can be a film director, rewinding the action and replaying different outcomes. Now that you are playing at being "lucid in this nightmare," you have many options.

You could ask a frightening dream figure why he is following you, or actively change the nightmare story so that something harmonious or amusing takes place. You could introduce help into the dream in the form of a strong friend, a magic tool, or a healing mantra. You could try passively reliving the nightmare free from fear and observe how this affects the imagery and events. The best nightmare solutions are not forced; allow the imagery to develop spontaneously in response to your initial guiding thought or question. You'll know when you've found the right nightmare solution because your tension around the dream will greatly diminish and you'll feel safe and calm.

5. Programme Yourself to Get Lucid

When you are happy with your nightmare solution, you are ready to return to sleep. This is an excellent time to watch as your hypnagogic imagery builds up into a moving dream and set a firm intention to fall asleep consciously. As you fall asleep, try repeating, "I am lucid, I am lucid ..." or "The next thing I see will be a dream."

The practice you have just done with the Lucid Imaging Nightmare Solution, observing and changing dream imagery in a relaxed, pre-sleep state, is a form of lucidity rehearsal that will help you to become lucid in your next dream. It is also useful to use this post-nightmare work to programme yourself to become lucid the next time you have a nightmare. Simply repeat, "The next time something bad happens, I'll recognise that I'm dreaming." When working with a recurrent nightmare, remind yourself that the next time you are confronted with its particular imagery, this will trigger lucidity.

⟨∽ *Practice 56* ∽⟩
Ten Nightmare Options for Use in Lucid Imaging and Lucid Dreaming

Any of the options available to you during the Lucid Imaging Nightmare Solution technique are of course also available to you during lucid trance states such as Lucid Writing, and during a lucid dream. For clarity, I've made a list of ten main actions you could find useful when faced with nightmare images or scary dream events in any state of consciousness. Choose your favourites, invent new ones, and discover which work best for you.

1. Call for Help

Ask the dream itself for help, but not in a shrieking, fearful way—state it as calmly as you can. "Send me help, please." *Expect* help to arrive in any form—it might be a dangling rope ladder to lift you away from the jaws of the monster, or a surprise superpower such as the ability to turn invisible or see through walls. A strong dream friend may leap to your rescue (hence the importance of making dream friends whenever we can).

2. Offer a Gift or Blow a Kiss

Everyone loves a gift, right? Sinister dream figures or snarling dream beasts are no exception. Reach into your pocket expecting the perfect gift to materialise, and see what comes out—a sapphire, a rubber duck? Doesn't really matter as long as it's offered with love. If you have no pocket or if nothing appears, try blowing the dream a kiss. This also works with frightening dream stories such as clinging to a piece of driftwood in a stormy ocean. We change the dream with our mindset. We blow a kiss of gratitude because for an instant we are enlightened—this nightmare is here to help us learn and grow on some level; how very kind of it! Our mood lifts, and the dream responds; the waves calm, or we are saved by a mermaid. Inevitably, there is a response. On the deepest level, the dream is us and we are the dream, which means that whether we like to think so or not, the nightmare is us and we are the nightmare!

3. Annihilation

Sometimes responding with love and compassion is the last thing on our minds. In some cases, it can be psychologically empowering to respond with force, particularly in the case of dreams that represent times in our life when we were victims of trauma, abuse, or bullying. This is a *dream*, so if we feel in the moment that what we really need to do is kick the shit out of a dream bully, that is our call.

I've said elsewhere that I don't see it as my role to judge people's dream behaviour. I do feel that a live dream friend is worth more than a dead dream enemy. My own experience is that responding to aggressive dream figures with forgiveness, love, and compassion results in the most mind-blowing integrative experiences I've had. The kind where I wake up buzzing with light and energy and bounce out of bed totally stoked, knowing that I've turned a dream enemy into a powerful dream friend.

4. Fearless Surrender

When we know we are dreaming, we can release all our fear. One possible response is to surrender to the nightmare—if a woolly mammoth is charging you, stay put and let it steamroll you flat or scoop you up with its tusks like a forklift truck. You may be surprised when it does neither of these things, but stops in front of you and raises its truck gently to your face to sniff you. You've found a new furry dream friend!

The fearless surrender option can and often does lead to incredible experiences of dissolving into light or being swept off into the sparkling multicoloured depths of the lucid void to receive knowledge. It's as if the dream notices our willingness to relinquish our ego and rewards us with spiritual gifts.

5. Become a Dream Magician

Dream magic is possible from any age. In one recurring nightmare, my four-year-old daughter faced scary witches. Instead of panicking, she magicked a little toy witch for them to play with—and the moment she gave it to them, it turned into an adorable live baby witch. The other witches were delighted! They all had a picnic together and the nightmare never returned. We are magicians in our lucid dreams (and in our waking imagination anything is possible too). We might choose to shoot globules of light at the scary elements in our dream, or swish our vanishing cloak over our heads and disappear, or whip up a storm to cause the vampire bats to retreat…it's fun to imagine all manner of magical possibilities during waking dream re-entries, and have them in mind when we become lucid in a nightmare.

6. Ask for a Gift

It may feel a bit cheeky to ask a flame-tongued, three-headed dream dragon for a gift, and you may end up with something you didn't expect (can a charred hole in the ground really be considered a gift?), but you might end up with something spectacularly useful—a turquoise gemstone for seeing into the future…or a fire-proof jumpsuit.

7. Turn into an Escape Artist

Sometimes we just want to get away from the nastiness of a nightmare, even if we know it could be beneficial to seize our courage in both hands and face our demons. Luckily, we have as many escape options as we like, including waking ourselves up by holding our breath and wiggling our toes. An escape artist might choose to outwit a dream aggressor in a dark alley by disappearing down a trap door or performing aerial flips like a prize-winning gymnast.

8. Build a Protective Shield

This is a useful protection to use any time you feel under threat, and can be done mentally in waking life situations too, when we are confronted by aggressive or tiresome people. Visualise yourself within an egg of protective white light. In dreams and visualisations, this can be reinforced with power gestures: push your arms outwards, upwards, and sideways to increase the protective light surrounding your body.

9. Ask the "Message" Question

Pausing in the fear and confusion of a nightmare to ask the dream figure, animal, or situation: "Do you have a message for me?" can have transformative results. A terrifying tidal wave may stop in its tracks to show you a close-up image of your bullying boss, conveying the message: your work situation is overwhelming you and big change is coming. A dream panther might respond, "I am here to give you my agility and fearlessness." Be prepared for the dream to surprise you with its response. One woman asked a giant man who was chasing her, "Why are you chasing me?" Seeming mortified, he shrank down to a normal size and told her sadly, "You need me for your fear!" It can be illuminating to realise that we are the creators of our fear. Crucially, this realisation enables us to release excess fear so that we free up energy for other areas of our life.

10. Hug the Monster

Nothing says that we have to hug an unpleasant element in our dream (what if it's a venomous sea urchin?). This option encompasses any loving gesture. We might send love and light by placing our hands over our heart and opening them towards the nightmare image. Hugging can be pretty amazing, though (and I imagine a dream sea urchin's spines and venom would dissolve during a lucid hug). A hug can be both welcoming and a kind of surrender. With a hug, we send this message to our inner monster: "I love and accept and welcome you into my heart. We are one." How beautiful is that? It's enough to bring a tear to the eye of the most hardened dream monster! A dream hug can be a fast and wonderful way to integrate rejected parts of ourselves and make a solid dream friend for the future.

––––––––––

The Lucid Imaging Nightmare Solution is excellent practice for lucid dreaming, as it helps us to rehearse possible actions and reactions that we can then put into practice in the dream state. If you practise any of the above responses mentally by closing your eyes and imagining them playing out positively in your latest bad dream, you'll send a powerful message to your dreaming mind that these are valid and effective responses in the face of fearsome dreams. You'll build a habit of responding with creativity, power, and compassion to nightmares. It will become natural even in your non-lucid dreams to respond to any threat with flexible action instead of terror. The following practice shows how to turn feelings of fear into lucidity triggers.

Anxiety, Unease, and Fear as Lucidity Triggers

Train yourself to become lucid in your nightmares. Any time you feel anxious, worried, or fearful while awake, take a moment to label the emotion: "I'm feeling anxious." Be mindful of this feeling of anxiety; notice where it is in your body. Is your belly tight? Is your head hurting? Then ask yourself, "Am I dreaming right now?"

Take a deep breath and do a quick reality check. This will calm you somewhat in your waking life situation, and if you do it often enough, it will create an automatic lucidity trigger that will carry over into your dreams. Building this kind of response while awake is so valuable because once it is integral and automatic for you to associate negative emotions with reality checks, you'll start to reap the benefits of this connection in your dreams. As soon as you experience fear or anxiety, you'll realise that you are *dreaming* this!

You'll find it much easier to liberate yourself from fear and anxiety once you recognise that you are in a dream and will wake up safely in your bed after this experience. You can then explore these feelings within the lucid dream state, or discover why the dream is bringing up these emotions. You'll soon become adept at recognising that you're dreaming and releasing fear to engage in creative and healing ways with the dream.

In time, you'll find that fear or anxiety will act as natural lucidity triggers. As soon as I get a serious feeling of unease in a dream, 90 percent of the time I automatically realise I'm dreaming. Knowing that we have an array of options helps us to create a happier dream life.

Sleep Paralysis

Have you ever had that awful, stuck-in-quicksand feeling in a dream? You're running from an attacker, but your limbs turn to stone; you struggle to move forward but it's impossible and he's gaining on you, his breath hot on the back of your neck… You wake up with a pounding heart and may still experience that heaviness in your limbs as you try to rouse yourself from your nightmare.

Why does this happen? Everyone experiences muscular paralysis during REM sleep. This is a biological safety mechanism to stop us from acting out our dreams and waking up with injuries from running into walls or falling down stairs. The muscles involved with breathing and our eye muscles are the only parts of our body that aren't paralysed.

This means that every night we experience "quicksand limbs," but we only notice it when we remain conscious during the transition from the waking state into sleep, or when we emerge consciously from REM sleep and feel stuck. The sensations of the dream body get mixed up with those of the physical body and this mixed up state can result in bizarre hallucinations and sensations such as being crushed or suffocated. This is known as sleep paralysis (SP), and understandably some people find it extremely frightening at first, until they learn how to respond.

Another unpleasant sleep event that often seems linked to sleep paralysis is the lucid nightmare. This happens when, even though we know we're dreaming, frightening things are happening and we can't wake ourselves up fully. Any panic we feel is bound to make the nightmare worse. In the lucid nightmare state, we are highly alert mentally, but we may experience "stuck" and "trapped" sensations because our dream body is getting all mixed up with our physical body as it lies in natural paralysis.

Yet despite the unpleasantness these states can bring, sleep paralysis can serve as a portal into lucid dreaming, and for that reason we can even learn to look forward to it and welcome it into our night of sleep! The following practice shares tips on how to relax into sleep paralysis and how to make the most of our lucidity during this weird transitional phase of sleep.

⟅∽ *Practice 58* ∽⟆
Sleep Paralysis Tricks

When we learn how to handle sleep paralysis, it can become a gift; a springboard to fantastic lucid adventures.

- Sleep paralysis is where we "wake up" mentally while our body is still paralysed and our dreaming mind is still switched on. This means *we are already lucidly aware* whenever we find ourselves in SP! We are mere moments away from lucid dreaming. That's already something to be happy about, so if you feel scared, just remind yourself that SP is a threshold to lucid dreaming.

- If scary things are happening, do not struggle. Struggling and fighting in sleep paralysis only makes it worse because it sends you into a flailing panic. Remind yourself that this is a transitional state of consciousness and congratulate yourself on your mental alertness and lucidity. Remind yourself that your body continues to sleep safely in your bed, and that you will wake up safely from this experience. Fear is your worst enemy in sleep paralysis, because this is a thought-responsive environment that will respond to your expectations as well as mirroring and amplifying your emotions. If you truly want out, hold your breath to shock your body into waking.

- Focus on calming your mind and releasing fear. It's helpful to practise a calming technique while awake, so that you can automatically use it when stuck in sleep paralysis. Try breathing in *calm* and breathing out *fear*. Any breathing technique can work wonders in sleep paralysis because it will calm your mind and simultaneously release the fear in your physical body. You could also create a protective shield of white light around your dream body. Try an affirmation: "I release all fear. I am always safe in the dream state." It's also effective to bring a memory of happiness and safety to mind and allow it to expand, filling your heart and mind.

- If you practise meditation, now is the time to test it in dream space. This can be incredible and lead you straight into deep lucid dreaming states of bliss.

- Be curious. Document events, imagery, and sensations like a scientist. Notice swooping or falling sensations, loud noises, voices, shadows moving in the space around you—but don't get drawn into feeling frightened or out of control. Remind yourself again that we all pass through sleep paralysis every night, we just don't usually notice it as we lose consciousness first. You are the lucid dreaming equivalent of an astronaut—an oneironaut. Imagine you have to report on this new dream space that you are discovering. What will you say? How will you describe it? This is a lucid adventure, a surreal interactive movie, a window into the dreaming mind. Enjoy your status as an intrepid explorer of dream space.

- Remind yourself that your physical body is paralysed but your dream body isn't—so try rubbing your dream hands together or performing a dream-body backflip. It can be easier in SP to stay asleep rather than wake up, since waking up involves battling through all the paralysis, numb limbs, strange sensations, and pins and needles that can occur on the road to waking up. And of course, if you're interested in having a lucid dream, you'll find it kind of helpful to stay asleep!

- If you are experiencing sleep paralysis hallucinations, practise the Lucid Imaging Nightmare Solution. No need to wait until you've woken up from this frightening sleep experience—there's no time like the present, so calm yourself with a deep breath and begin the steps. Think back to the moment when you became fearful (the "tipping point") and start working to restore the balance. You can interact calmly and creatively with whatever is happening right now in your sleep paralysis. If there's a glowing-eyed demon crouching in the corner of your bedroom, use any of the ten nightmare options listed in Practice 56. You might ask the demon for a gift or if it has a message for you. You might send it love and light (recognising that it is part of you and cannot harm you, and that you will soon wake up safely in your bed).

- Create a lucid dream by visualising a gorgeous, inviting scene. Does your fantasy scene involve rowing a wooden boat on a sparkling lake? Snowboarding down a mountain? Bring your scene to vivid life and roll, slide, or melt into it while staying consciously aware. You're lucid dreaming!

Navigating sleep paralysis can take courage initially, and a certain amount of perseverance, but it can quickly become an arena for honing your Lucid Imaging Nightmare Solution skills, and a welcome stepping stone to lucid dreaming. Our assumptions about dream figures may also need to be examined carefully as we learn to respond calmly to sleep paralysis, as shown in the next practice.

Ↄ⌒◌ *Practice 59* ◌⌒Ↄ
How to Relax Around Frightening Dream Figures

It can be helpful to question your beliefs about what happens in sleep paralysis and lucid nightmares.

- Ask yourself: "Do I see frightening dream figures as separate from me?" If so, you are giving those dream figures power. Historically, people believed that sleep paralysis experiences were supernatural visits, which of course made them even more terrifying! Today, we know that as the body transitions into sleep, our brain, physical body, and sensory perceptions go through changes that can result in crazy sensations if we stay conscious while they happen. Use this knowledge to help you to release fear of any spooky figures you meet in SP so you can brave the ride.

- Ask yourself: "Are dream figures, whether nice or nasty, part of myself? Are they part of the collective unconscious?" When we take the attitude that dream figures have turned up in our dream to teach us something or illuminate something for us, we are much more likely to get the most out of our nightmares. This is not to say that this is the "right" thing to believe. Naturally, it's up to each individual to draw their own conclusions about the nature of the people and animals they meet in their dreams.

- Unpleasant or scary dream figures might represent past trauma or they may mirror difficult feelings we have about a current situation in our lives. They might appear as a reminder that we need to learn new ways to react to threats or pressure. While many dream figures seem to reflect our personal lives or unacknowledged "shadow" aspects of our own personality, others may be transpersonal, symbolising the state of our planet or the cosmos. In the case of dark presences in sleep paralysis, these may arise solely from the uneasy overlap between the dream body and the physical body that occurs in sleep paralysis. The dreaming mind has an unparalleled talent for turning physical sensations directly into super-realistic and highly emotive imagery.

- Release fear, be curious, and fill your heart with love—this is the attitude that gets us the furthest when it comes to ominous dream figures. There's a simple equation in the dream world that you'll notice I keep returning to: when we change our attitude towards frightening dream figures, *they change in response.* Be strong, claim your own power, and don't let fear be your master. Who knows, you may even make a new friend. And after this dream, *you will wake up safely in your bed!*

———————

In this chapter, we've explored the way that our own fear can impact dreams and rapidly turn them into nightmares. We've seen how Lucid Writing and the Lucid Imaging Nightmare Solution can help us to resolve unpleasant dreams by asking questions of the dream and creating flexible responses to fearful situations. We've looked at the healing power of changing bad dreams into good ones. I've shared tips for responding to scary sleep paralysis experiences and shown how to turn them into lucid dreams. We've seen how to react to frightening dream figures and explored the value of reacting with curiosity and love in the face of aggressive dream animals and people.

When we work lucidly with nightmares, either during or after the dream, we can help ourselves move from fear to healing, and this empowers us to unwrap the precious gifts that nightmares hold. The next chapter looks into the healing and creative possibilities of lucid dreaming.

CHAPTER 9

Going Deeper: Creativity,
Healing, and Spiritual
Lucid Experiences

When we manage to get lucid, stay lucid, and grow familiar with the basic laws of the lucid dream world, we are in a position to go deeper into lucid dreaming. As we do so, we inevitably learn a lot about our motivations, reactions, expectations, and desires. There's usually no escaping ourselves when lucid in a dream for two reasons. Firstly, because we *are* the lucid dream and it is us. Secondly, because dreams respond instantly to our thoughts and intentions in surprising, creative ways—which is why it's so much fun to guide dreams! However, in deep lucid dreaming, we can "escape" our ego-selves when our dream body dissolves along with our self-concept and we experience ourselves as pure, disembodied, conscious awareness. Are you intrigued? This chapter explores how to have this amazing deep lucid dreaming experience and how to go deeper in other ways.

We'll look at how lucid dreaming enables us to engage consciously with powerful dream imagery to promote creativity, healing, and spiritual experiences. We'll examine how to heal physical and psychological issues in lucid dreams, and I'll share tips on what to expect when weird dream stuff happens and you find yourself floating lucidly in infinite blackness (the lucid void), shooting out of your body amidst noisy buzzing vibrations (out-of-body experience), or encountering blissful light in a state of pure awareness (the Lucid Light).

Let's begin by looking at how we can enhance and deepen our creativity to access original ideas and artistic inspiration.

Creative Lucid Dreaming: Connect with Your Inner Artist

Creativity is not reserved only for a select few artists and writers—we are *all* creative, and if anyone is in doubt about this, I warmly invite them to look to their dreams! This is where we encounter the mind in its most creative form. The visions experienced in dreams are multi-sensory, three-dimensional, and emotionally charged. They can change as fast as thought, and in response to thought. Dreams are pure creative energy. Every night, our dreaming mind releases this wildly creative stream of images, emotions, associations, memories, ideas, and imaginings. All of life is present in our dreams, and we can connect to the deep, rich resources of our unconscious by waking up in our dreams.

During the writing of my first novel, *Breathing in Colour*, I got stuck on the voice of one of the main characters, a teenaged girl called Mia. She needed to be different in some way, but I couldn't get it right. Every time I wrote in her voice, it came out wooden and rigid, nothing like what I wanted. Then I had a lucid dream where I was lying on a beach and I knew without looking that the sand in my fist was luminous orange, because *I could feel the orangeness through the pores of my dream skin.*

When I awoke from this unusual lucid dream, I did some online searching and discovered synaesthesia. This is a sensory condition where musical notes might be experienced as having different flavours or colours felt as sensations on the skin. After that lucid dream, I knew that Mia was a synaesthete. My creative block dissolved in the blink of an eye. I had further lucid dreams where I deliberately invoked synaesthesia to help me write in Mia's voice. The result was rich, multi-sensory, imaginative writing that I had never produced before.

In lucid dreams, we can experience sensations and events that we have never experienced before in waking life. Take floating, for example. Or flying Superman-style. How often in waking life have we jumped into the air and floated effortlessly upwards? The closest experience would be diving to the bottom of a swimming pool and pushing up lightly. And as for flying like Superman, many of us have done it virtually, by projecting our imagination into simulated computer games, but who has actually felt the sensation of flying alone through the sky unaided by equipment? In dreams, we can do this and feel our skin tingling as we zoom along. Such experiences can be translated into art or expressed through music.

In lucid dreams, we wake up inside this hyper-realistic, naturally creative environment. Imagine swooping down a ski slope at breakneck speed, knowing you can't hurt yourself as this is a dream, and then bringing this experience to life on the page of your novel-in-progress. Or sitting in a dream bar with one of your screen idols and getting acting tips and advice from them. Or becoming lucid and asking the dream for help with your business plan, exam question, or scientific invention. The deep creativity of dreams, combined with lucidity and after-the-dream techniques such as Lucid Writing, can lead to new ideas, astonishing leaps in understanding, and problem-solving.

Freedom unlocks creativity, and so does the delicate balance of conscious and unconscious in lucid dreaming. Lucid dreamers can tap into the teeming creativity of the unconscious and guide this creative source to help them in specific ways: a sculptor might ask the dream to take them to a garden filled with original sculpture; a surgeon might practise operations in lucid dreams; or a fiction writer could choose to invent a story. It can also be helpful for us to use lucid dream creativity to improve physical skills—one guy swam through honey in his lucid dreams to test the muscle resistance as he practised his swim stroke; a woman sparred with a flexi-glass version of herself while lucid dreaming as she needed a sparring partner her own size to practise with. When we become lucid (and stable) in a dream, truly we have an inexhaustible creative source at our fingertips.

In one lucid dream, I wanted to explore how to develop a fictional plot, so I turned myself into a fairy tale princess and let the story unfold, with the full knowledge that I was the producer, director, and actress all rolled into one. It turned into an exciting story which ended with me taking possession of some magical gemstones and the fire brigade busting down the castle door because they wanted the gems! As the door crashed open, with supreme lucid concentration I caused myself to disappear atom by atom—something I'd never tried in a dream before.

Creative lucid trances were covered in chapter 6, so this next practice focuses on what we can do to trigger creative outcomes, new ideas, and original artistic creations while lucid in a dream.

Practice 60
Lucid Dreaming for Deeper Creativity

When we wake up in a dream, we encounter the rampant creativity of the unconscious mind with full conscious awareness. This leads to transformative, spontaneous creative inspiration.

- *Try something new:* In dreams, we are less inhibited. When we become lucid, we can try out any art form with full awareness but without fear of failure. A new dance routine; an oil painting; rock music; the Tai Chi form; parachute jumping; spontaneous poetry. We can practise a business talk or a kick-boxing manoeuvre … or combine these two things, just for fun!

  In dreams, anything can happen. Once, I practised the art of glassblowing. It was incredible because the coloured molten glass behaved like giant soap bubbles, wobbling up into the air above me. One multi-coloured glass bubble was the size of a bus! It was unexpected, pure dream creativity, and an absolute marvel to behold.

- *Ask the dream to help you and it will respond:* In a lucid dream, I asked "Show me something creative!" and spotted a big treasure chest lolling open behind a tree. Inside were colourful materials—ribbons, wool, glitter, shells, silk strips, and so on. Beautiful! I ran my fingers through their rich textures. When I woke up, I was inspired to create a multimedia collage using all these materials for the first time.

  In an interesting twist, I should tell you that the treasure chest was guarded by two big dogs! Often, we need to overcome inner obstacles or hidden doubts before we dare to diversify into a new art form. But that's okay, because we can be brave in lucid dreams, if we choose to be. When I faced those dogs with fearless lucidity, they ran off and left me to discover my creative treasures.

• *Stay flexible:* If you try to force waking life creativity, it often responds by shutting down. It can be the same in a lucid dream. Go with the flow while keeping your goal in mind, and the rewards will be rich. React creatively to obstacles within your dream—what if you come up against a brick wall? Well, why not take the opportunity to explore lucid dream physics and the nature of the lucid dream body? In 2013, I wrote in my dream journal: "Lucid, I press my whole body through a wall very slowly to experience it atom by atom. It's like moving through semi-hardened glue."

• *Observe the dream as it creates itself:* Simply standing still when you become lucid and watching the dream as it continues around you can be an awesome experience. It's like watching a film of your mind at play. Look out for glimpses of amazing creativity as the dream breathes life into every tiny detail within it, from a blade of grass quivering in the breeze to the peculiar purple pelicans flying above your head.

• *Give an initial impetus:* If you want to guide the dream towards a specific creative project, make a verbal request when you get lucid ("How should my finished sculpture look?"). Then relax, wait expectantly, and see how the dream responds. Anything could happen—a brick wall might explode to reveal a gleaming pink Cadillac, or a hole right through the core of the earth might appear. Be ready, hold your hat on, and stay lucid!

• *Work on a nightmare:* When people with creative blocks tell me that they only have a "dream scrap" to work with, I always say, "Well, that's okay because you can get a lot out of a dream scrap." If they tell me they "only" have a nightmare to work with, I feel a leap of excitement, because I know that this will generate deep creativity for sure. A nightmare is compressed creative energy! Free that energy in a lucid dream by using the techniques in chapter 8, or work on it while awake, and your art will transform.

Now let's look at what may be the ultimate creative expression: healing.

How Does Emotional and Physical
Lucid Dream Healing Work?

As we go through life, all of us experience various degrees of emotional trauma. These can range from isolated upsetting events to the grief of losing a loved one. Such experiences may be reflected in our dreams in the form of anxious dream scenarios, dreams with strong negative emotional content, or recurring nightmares. As we explored in the nightmare chapter, all dreams come to help and heal us, even nightmares, which can be seen as red flags that cry out to us, "Healing is needed!" Lucidity can help us gain insight into emotional issues or resolve them. Lucid dreaming is a thought-responsive environment, so our intent can have a transformative effect on the dream.

One young man had a serious fear of the dark. He had nightmares about a demonic cupboard, until in a lucid dream he decided to face his fears. The cupboard shook as if something was about to burst out if it, but he kept walking toward it and it dissolved into shreds of shadow. Beyond it he saw sunlit fields and walked into them. From that day on, he was no longer scared of the dark. Facing a phobia takes courage—but lucid dreaming can help us face our fears.

When we direct healing intent in the dream, by choosing to face our fears, or by sending love and light to negative dream people or events, the imagery may change spontaneously into something healing. When healing change takes place on the level of the unconscious, we experience inner resolution, and the wonderful thing is that *outer change* then naturally follows this and we feel the positive effects in our waking lives.

Any state of consciousness where we actively mingle waking and dreaming consciousness has enormous transformative potential! Lucidity gives us insight into emotional blocks and deep-rooted fears and can trigger powerful healing. I'm not a big fan of mathematics, but there's one equation I love to use:

Lucidity + Dream Imagery = Transformation

The same equation can also be applied when we work lucidly to heal physical ailments and illness. There is a growing number of anecdotal reports from lucid dreamers who claim to have healed physical complaints ranging from inflamed tendons to benign tumours to tinnitus (ringing of the ears) by directing healing intent toward their complaint while lucid in a dream.

Anyone who has woken from a scary dream with unmissable physical sensations of fear, such as a racing heart and clammy hands, has experienced the mind-body connection. Dreams can sometimes warn us of physical disease, as shown by studies into breast cancer warning dreams. One lady was even able to show her doctor the exact place beneath her breast where he needed to insert the biopsy needle, because a dream showed her where the cancerous lump was situated. The doctor did what she said—and found an aggressive, fast-moving cancer right in that spot.[18] Reports of warning health dreams are relatively common. Another woman dreamed she had a glowing blue egg at the base of her skull and knew it was a tumour. Tests showed that she did indeed have a brain tumour in that spot.[19]

Our dreaming mind translates physical sensations directly into imagery. But please don't imagine that every dream you have is a doom-laden health message! Most dreams are emotional rather than physical, so even the strongest nightmare may have absolutely nothing to do with physical health, nor warn of a grim future. The best way to discover the meaning of your dream is to unwrap its message using practical tools such as the ones I share in *Dream Therapy*.

The mind can alter unconscious body processes, as seen in hypnosis, where healing suggestions are made in a light trance and healing imagery is developed to overlay old, negative patterns of imagery. When we work directly with the imagery-rich language of the unconscious and enable it to change in healing ways, we can have a powerful effect on our state of health. In a lucid dream, rather than lying drowsily on a couch in light hypnosis, we are fully immersed in the vivid, all-encompassing world of dream imagery. This, combined with our alert state of awareness, creates a powerful combination for healing. Lucid dreamer Dr. Beverly D'Urso had a uterine cyst and a mass that doctors suspected might be a tumour. She experienced a lucid dream healing in which colourful geometric figures in the sky beamed healing

---

18. Burk. "Warning Dreams Preceding the Diagnosis of Breast Cancer." 134.

19. Mallon. *Dreams, Counselling and Healing.* 101.

energy onto her. The next day, an ultrasound scan showed no cyst, no possible mass, and a healthy uterus.[20]

Scientific research studies show that actions carried out in a dream have a measurable effect on the physical body. Lucid dreamers can affect their heartrate, breathing, and muscle tone. Neuroscientists have shown that when lucid dreamers clench their fists, the same part of their brain lights up as when they clench their fists while awake.[21] Sport psychologists have concluded that athletes can improve their physical performance by practising in their lucid dreams.[22]

Most people readily agree that lucid dreaming can help with *emotional* issues. Yet despite these illuminating studies into the connection between dream actions and the physical body, some find it hard to accept that we can draw on the power of the dreaming mind to heal the *physical* body. What's your view on this? My suggestion, as always, is to keep an open mind, create your own experiments, and find out for yourself in your own lucid dreams. The following two practices aim to give you a platform from which you may launch yourself into whichever aspect of lucid dream healing—emotional or physical—you would most like to explore.

৩৩ *Practice 61* ৩৩
How to Trigger Emotional Healing in Lucid Dreams

When we are able to calm our emotions and stabilise the lucid dream, we are in an excellent position to work in healing ways with even the most disturbing imagery.

- In the face of scary or unhealthy dream imagery (a menacing ghost, a vat of acid) create a protective egg of light around you or recite a mantra. Calm yourself. Stabilise lucidity using the CLEAR technique and prepare to take healing action. Below are different ways of reacting to unpleasant dream imagery in healing ways. Choose your favourite or create your own and practise it mentally during a pre-sleep visualisation to get used to it and play with possible healing effects.

---

20. Johnson, *Llewellyn's Complete Book of Lucid Dreaming*. 275.
21. Dresler et al., "Dreamed Movement Elicits Activation in the Sensorimotor Cortex."
22. Erlacher et al., "Frequency of Lucid Dreams and Lucid Dream Practice in German Athletes."

- The goal is not to "whitewash" negative dream imagery. The dream is an honest mirror that can show us not only what we're feeling or dealing with, but how to find a way through to healing and empowerment. Forcing the dream imagery into something more palatable likely won't result in deep healing. Instead, remain calm, open, curious, and compassionate, as this enables spontaneous change and deeper healing.

- Create a feeling of love in your heart and send love and light to any frightening or distressing dream imagery, people, or animals. This is much more powerful and helpful than trying to force change.

- Ask the dream questions: *Why is this dream unfolding like this? Is there a message for me? I am open to hearing the message of this dream. I am open to healing in this dream.* Seek understanding. Why is this dream occurring now? Consider this lucidly. With insight comes spontaneous healing.

- Present a menacing dream figure or snarling dream animal with a gift. Surprise them! Their reaction may well surprise you in return.

- Ask yourself, "What do I need to feel safe in this situation?" I always tell my young daughter, "Whenever you ask for help in a dream, help will arrive." This is the truth … if you believe that it is. And belief plays a huge role in the healing process and in lucid dreaming, too. Children believe the trusted adults in their life. When they carry into the dream the belief that help is at hand, lo and behold, help manifests! Help arrives in the form of a rescue helicopter, a muscular friend, a defending animal. Adults sometimes have to relearn that trusting spirit. Help yourself to feel safe in your dreams by summoning help. Trust and expect that it will arrive.

Now let's look at how to heal physical issues in lucid dreams.

⟳ *Practice 62* ⟲
Lucid Dream Healing of Physical Ailments
Light, love, and lucidity are the three magic "L" words when it comes to healing. When we manage to combine them, we stand a good chance of easing

physical aches and pains and creating a valuable new "picture of health" to bring back to waking life with us.

- To heal a physical ailment, direct healing energy towards the affected part of your body with a gesture, such as placing your hand there or extending your fingers.
- Create a healing ball of light: rub your palms together in the dream and feel healing energy grow between them. You may see warm light or sparks between your hands. Apply this healing energy to your body.
- Remember, you don't need to touch the afflicted part of your body to heal it—you don't even need to be in your dream body! The power of healing intent is strong in any state of consciousness, but in a lucid dream it can be particularly powerful. Use your lucid intent to beam healing to yourself on all levels.
- Trust your intuition—stay flexible to how the dream unfolds once you have brought into it the intention to heal.
- Love is an incredibly healing energy. Summon love in your heart, place your hands on your heart, and then send that love to whatever ails you.
- Within the lucid dream, visualise yourself in vibrant health. This creates a strong new mental image for you to internalise on a profound unconscious level.
- Create a healing mantra and sing your healing song at the top of your lucid lungs, causing the entire dream to reverberate with healing sound energy. This can be incredibly exhilarating.

These healing actions may spontaneously integrate and transform unhealthy imagery. Black fungus may react to healing intent by turning into a carpet of spring flowers. An aggressive dog might turn into a playful one. You may wake up feeling the physical and emotional effects of your healing intent. Remember: your dreaming mind wants you to heal! Healing is always available to us in the dream state.

Spiritual Lucid Dreaming

We've looked at emotional and physical healing. Now we'll look at spiritual or soul healing in lucid dreams. People report encounters with deities, religious presences, and spiritual gurus in their lucid dreams. One woman saw a field full of Buddha statues that she suddenly realised were alive and breathing! Another often floats on what she describes as "the luminous winds of the Holy Spirit." It also seems common for people to experience profound states of bliss while lucid in dreams, and these often involve dissolving into light.

Have you ever had a dream where the imagery falls away and you find yourself floating in what seems like infinite space? Light is often present in accounts of healing and in spiritual encounters. I came up with the term "Lucid Light"[23] after experiencing this all-encompassing, soul-nourishing light in deep lucid dreams. Such experiences are nothing new and have been reported across cultures and religions that span millennia, but their commonness doesn't mean it isn't deeply marvellous and spiritually refreshing to experience them. The Lucid Light can help not only with spiritual and emotional healing, but with physical healing. After an operation to remove a cancerous tumour, one man kept finding himself floating in a cube of white light in his lucid dreams. He knew he was being healed in these dreams, and made a good recovery.

After hundreds of encounters with blissful light sources in lucid dreams as well as in meditative and trance states, I consider the Lucid Light to be our baseline state of consciousness, the ever-present source light of conscious awareness that we all emerge from at birth and return to when we die. Lucid Light dreams tend to involve luminescence of any colour, or black light, and are often accompanied by the experience of expanding into oneness.

We can encounter the Lucid Light in any state of consciousness, but it seems especially easy to reach it in lucid dreams, out-of-body experiences, the pre-sleep hypnagogic state, highly lucid waking moments, during meditation, while floating in the sparkling black lucid void, and in luminous dreams. Reports of near-death experiences often mention soulful, magnificent light. This light is with us (and within us) all the time, it's just a case of knowing how to reach it. Lucid Light experiences can be so utterly and profoundly amazing

---

23. Johnson, *Sleep Monsters and Superheroes.*

that they revitalise and refresh us to our very core. These experiences can help with anxiety, depression, and burnout.

Once, I finished a stressful book deadline and collapsed onto my bed, totally drained and beginning to feel physically ill. Instantly, the room filled up with luminescence; a warm, golden light that felt so welcome and supportive as it encompassed my body. I floated blissfully within it, fully aware. I couldn't feel my body anymore. I surrendered to the incredible sensation of floating in pure, healing light. After a time, my eyes opened and I saw that I'd been in that state of bliss for ninety minutes. No dreams, only Lucid Light. I sat up and was astonished at how energised I felt. I bounced out of bed, grabbed my mountain bike, and went for a long, riverside bike ride, feeling on top of the world. Talk about a power nap—that was a battery recharge plugged right into the energy source. I glowed like a 100-watt lightbulb!

Spiritual lucid dreams of all types are treasures, and we tend to wake up from them with an inner glow. Let's look at how to stoke our spiritual fire by invoking them.

⊙⊸ *Practice 63* ⊶⊙
Get Lucid, Get Spiritual:
How to Invoke Spiritual Experiences

Whether we're atheists or religious, lucid dreaming can lead to blissful transcendental experiences that remain with us for a lifetime.

- *Set an intention.* Practise visualising yourself encountering the deity of your choice in your next lucid dream, or having an immersive experience of the Lucid Light. Create a mantra or a verbal request to use when you become lucid: "I am open to a spiritual/transcendent experience" or, "Take me to the Buddha" or, "I am divine light."

- *Move towards the light.* In any lucid dream and in other lucid states of consciousness, follow the light! You may be in a dream and see a particularly vibrant tree, or an object that has a glow to it, such as a luminous moon. Go to the tree and hug it or reach for the moon. Notice luminosity and recognise it for what it is: an especially aware part of your dream, one that could act as a portal into a deeper spiritual experience. Don't be shy about connecting with the light in your dreams, just be calm and respectful.

- *Meditate in your next lucid dream.* This is the fastest way to reach a state of bliss. With no physical body to distract us with aches and pains, in a lucid dream we go deep quickly and this can lead to wonderful experiences of oneness, interconnection, and compassion. No need to sit cross-legged if you don't want to—the intention to meditate, along with closing your eyes, should be enough to send you into a deep meditative state almost instantly. It helps, of course, if you have some experience with waking meditation.

- *Backflip into the divine.* When you become lucid and the dream is stable, float up into the air, then close your eyes and do a backflip (it's possible to perform this acrobatic feat with great elegance and grace in a dream—try it!) with the firm intention of moving directly into a divine encounter, or a spiritual or transcendent space. Use your mantra and release all fear, knowing that after this powerful experience *you will wake up safely in your bed.*

  Before that though, things may get exciting. You might find yourself pulled along through black, rushing winds, or sucked through rainbow tunnels of light. This is all fine—go with the flow, stay curious and aware. In many such lucid dreams, I get "spat out" at the end of one of these wormholes and that's when things get deep fast. It's like being a dream astronaut (an oneironaut) floating in vast space, weightless and aware, looking into infinity—pinpricks of coloured light, as if all the stars in the universe are around you. In this state it's common to no longer have a dream body but to experience yourself as a pinprick of awareness, and eventually even that sense of self may dissolve into an experience of profound peace and oneness.

- *Ask the dream probing existential questions.* These often lead to spontaneous and enlightening experiences like the one described in the previous point. In one lucid dream, I asked: "What are dreams made of?" The dream scene began to vibrate with incredible energy. I laughed, as this was such a familiar response to me. "Okay," I said, "I get it—dreams are made from energy! But tell me this then—what is *energy* made from?" The vibrations calmed down and these beautiful chains of light appeared; they linked together in intricate patterns until there was more and more light. In awe, I said, "Oh, wow! *Energy is made of light!*"

This lucid dream turned spontaneously into a powerful revelation, one that shaped my Lucid Light theory and inspired me to connect with the light in my dreams whenever I could. Questions to try (if you feel ready to hear the answers!) are: "What is my life's purpose?" "What happens after death?" Or try requests: "Show me my soul." "Show me my death." "Show me my future soulmate/child."

To complete this chapter, I'll briefly address two common experiences that often confuse and distress people when they first arise: the lucid void and out-of-body experiences.

The Lucid Void

In the lucid void, you're basically already in the Lucid Light, it's just black (or white, or multi-coloured) light; the gap between dreams, the stuff that dreams are made from! Once you find yourself here, all you need is the right mindset. This is one of calm lucidity, meditative alertness, and peaceful stillness.

I get messages from people asking me: "How can I escape from this terrible black space? I can't see anything and it scares me!" Well, as we've explored in this book, dreams are thought-responsive spaces, so if we feel horrified to find ourselves in the lucid void, it will likely be a horrifying experience!

It's like the story of the puppy who ran into a cave of mirrors—there he found a whole gang of puppies all looking right at him. Terrified, he barked—and all of them barked right back at him! Out he raced, his tail between his legs. Silence fell in the cave. His curiosity got the better of him and he ventured back inside, feeling calm and brave. To his delight, he met a whole crowd of calm puppies. He wagged his tail—and they all wagged their tails back at him! This is how it works in the lucid void and in any dream state. If you are having fearful dream experiences, work on calming your fear by day, by practising deep breathing, surrounding yourself in a protective egg of light, and reminding yourself, "I am safe." Bring this serenity into the lucid void with you, and your experience will transform in positive ways.

We are in control of our reactions to situations. We can learn to calm ourselves and cultivate an attitude of curiosity.

⚬⚬ *Practice 64* ⚬⚬
How to Release Fear and Respond in the Lucid Void

The lucid void is a wonderous state, one of infinite creative potential. Instead of fearing it and doing all we can to escape from it, it makes so much more sense to learn how to navigate it and explore its marvellous gifts.

- Practise calming techniques during the day, as described above, or recall a moment in your life when you felt totally safe and loved. Allow this feeling of wellbeing to envelop you. Chant "om" in the void to create a sensation of calm and send marvellous sound vibrations throughout the space.

- Welcome the void. It's a place of contemplation, painlessness, and infinite creativity. If it bothers you that you can only see blackness, create some light! There is light everywhere in the void, just look for it. At first you may see pinpricks of colour, or whole swathes of glowing light.

- If you are falling through the void, know that there is no rough landing awaiting you—these sensations are often caused when the brain transitions from the state of waking to the sleep state (hence the term, "falling asleep"). Simply relax and fall, perhaps trying out a few acrobatic feats on the way down.

- Play with your dream body if you have one. Stretch to become as long as a ladder or as wide as a house. You have an incredibly flexible dream body, so have some fun with it: try somersaults or impossible yoga poses. Be playful in the void. Make yourself chuckle—laughter is the best antidote to fear.

- Build up an orchestra of musical instruments or sing your heart out and observe the way sound causes the void to vibrate beautifully.

- Create a new dream—visualise anything you like and watch as the dream assembles itself before your eyes. This is fascinating; it sometimes appears as swirls of energy and colour that coalesce into dream people or full-blown scenes.

- Seek out the void whenever you get lucid. Once, I was testing how hard or easy it was to read text in a lucid dream when I read something that reminded me to head into a more expansive state:

I see the words: "Lucid dream expansion," and I like that. "Good idea," I think, "I'll let this lucid dream expand." I soar high into the air and the dream scene vanishes: I am in expansive darkness. I float bodiless in this vast, drifting space, the lucid void. It's like being among restful black clouds—I've fallen into the gap between dreams again. So peaceful…

Now that we've looked at the value of releasing fear in the lucid void and enjoying ourselves instead, let's take a look at out-of-body experiences, where the same principles apply.

Out-of-Body Experiences (OBE)

A common question I hear is: *"I've heard lucid dreaming is the same as having an out-of-body experience. But the idea terrifies me—what if I leave my body and never return?"* Firstly, lucid dreaming is not the same as an out-of-body experience (OBE). There are overlaps in how these states feel, but lucid dreaming happens only during sleep, whereas an OBE can happen during sleep, but it can also happen while we are wide awake. An OBE can be triggered by physical trauma, such as a car accident or fainting, or it can happen from a state of deep emotional shock. OBEs can even be caused using virtual technology to trigger a perceptual leap into a virtual body.

Secondly, you won't "leave your body and never return." If this were the case, millions of people of all ages and states of health would be found dead in their beds without any discernible cause. We have such a strong connection to the physical body. I know people who spend years and years trying to increase the frequency of their out-of-body experiences, and they really have to work at it. Others experience OBEs naturally and effortlessly (or even unwillingly, because they just happen). The entry into an OBE can be pretty crazy the first time it happens, as common sensations involve loud buzzing, strong vibrations, and then being propelled out of your physical body. Not all OBEs are this dramatic, though, and some people only become aware that they are having an OBE once they're already floating on the ceiling.

As with the lucid void, if you find yourself leaving your body, stay calm, curious, and aware, and enjoy the ride! Despite some fears around OBEs, they are perfectly natural and can be wonderful in terms of creativity, healing, and spiritual experiences. Many people seek out this experience, so this final practice aims to help you trigger an OBE from different states of consciousness.

ꙮꙮ *Practice 65* ꙮꙮ
How to Trigger an Out-of-Body Experience from a Lucid Dream and from Waking

When we relinquish fear around the idea of "leaving our body"—which is something we all do each night anyway, when we transition into a dream body—we open fabulous new possibilities for consciousness exploration.

- Visualise yourself leaving your physical body effortlessly. See the part of yourself that is pure light slip easily upwards and float or fly wherever you want to go. This is the first step in communicating to your unconscious mind your wish to have an OBE. Meditate with this visualisation and try it each time you find yourself in a deeply relaxed state, such as in the middle of the night after a mini-awakening.

- Daydream whenever you can about what you'll do when you leave your body.

- Next time you get lucid in a dream, ask the dream for help: "Please help me to have an OBE." Or be assertive: "OBE now!" It is possible to trigger an OBE from the dream state.

- While lucid dreaming, set the rock-solid intention to experience an OBE. Then zoom very fast upwards, through the ceiling, through the roof, through the clouds, through the earth's atmosphere, and right up into outer space and beyond. In my experience, this trick usually results in the dissolution of the dream body and the transformation into a bodiless streak of light.

- During the day, lie down and relax deeply, then visualise a strong rope dangling from the ceiling. Mentally grab onto it and easily pull yourself up it, hand over hand. Feel yourself leaving your physical body as you do so. Experience the immense freedom of floating, weightless, in your room. Then imagine flying outside into the warm sun and exploring. As you vividly imagine this experience on the cusp of sleep, you may start to feel vibrations or hear buzzing sounds. Relax into these, trusting this experience, and roll out of your body for real.

In this final chapter of the book, we've explored how to go deeper into lucid dreaming in the areas of creativity, healing, and spiritual or transcendent experiences. We've looked at the power of emotional and physical healing in lucid dreams. We've played with different possibilities for receiving creative inspiration and interacting creatively in our lucid dreams to bring new ideas to light. We've touched on the deep lucid dreaming state of Lucid Light and seen how blissful and revitalising this experience can be. We've examined ways of releasing fear when we find ourselves floating in the lucid void or having an out-of-body experience. I've shared practical tips ranging from how to invoke spiritual lucid dreams to how to trigger OBEs.

This is just the tip of the iceberg of what is possible when we go deeper into lucid dreaming! Deep lucid dreaming is an ocean, a whole other world to explore.

Conclusion

Lucidity is awareness. When we bring awareness to any aspect of our life, we enable transformation. Paying mindful attention to dreams and approaching lucid dreaming with curiosity and wonder can help us to become more aware and connected in our waking lives as well as in our dreams.

In *The Art of Lucid Dreaming*, we've discovered ourselves to be highly individual dreamers and sleepers. We've learned how to create a tailor-made, flexible Unique Lucidity Programme to reflect our personal path into lucid dreaming. It's good to revisit this programme regularly to change and refresh it, avoiding overfamiliarity with it at all costs because that's when boredom sneaks in, and boredom is a lucidity killer. When we keep things fresh and tickle our curiosity with new techniques, our interest remains high. All the practices in this book can be seen as recipes to tweak creatively to suit our own preferences, because the more personalised a technique is, the more effective it becomes.

The next steps are to keep practising, by day and by night!

We've looked at the power of intent, clarity, and expectation and how to take practical steps to get and stay lucid before guiding dreams in a range of creative and interactive ways. We've encountered nightmares, sleep paralysis, out-of-body experiences, and the lucid void, and stepped closer to our own dream people and animals. We've explored various lucid states that interconnect with lucid dreaming, from waking dreamwork such as Lucid Writing to the pre-sleep state of lucid hypnagogia and transcendental Lucid Light states. Each of these states can help us on many levels: creativity, healing, and self-understanding, as well as on the soul level of expanding our natural compassion and deepening the knowledge we have of ourselves as spiritual beings.

And there is so much more to discover! Beyond the pages of this practical book, a whole dazzling inner world awaits us all. One of the things I love about lucid dreaming is that it never loses its power to wow me. After more than forty years of personal lucid dream exploration, twenty-five years of studying it, and fifteen years of teaching the benefits of lucid dreaming to others, I am still awed by the discoveries that people make when they dive into their lucid dreams with courage, curiosity, and wonder.

One lady who was distraught over the sudden death of her father saw him in a lucid dream. He was radiant and happy. They hugged and she woke up feeling a sense of acceptance that had not been possible for her before. A soldier told me about the post-combat PTSD nightmares that he bravely managed to face through lucid dreaming. A young woman shared a transformative lucid dream in which she saw herself and her life from a higher perspective and felt intense love and compassion, understanding that she was doing her best in life and everything would turn out all right. A dying woman's spiritual experiences of dissolving into light in her lucid dreams helped her to face her imminent death with peace and equanimity.

The bravery and spirit of intrepid lucid dream explorers never fails to move me. This is such a wonderful state of consciousness with incredible potential for creativity, healing, spiritual growth, and philosophical expansion. We help ourselves and others on all levels when we discover the art of lucid dreaming.

But in the rush to chase the holy grail of lucid dreaming, let's not dismiss our non-lucid dreams. All dreams have value, even the scraggiest scrap of a dream, and all dreams have lucid potential. When we pay attention to every kind of dream we have, regardless of "how lucid" we were in it, we are paying attention to the deepest part of ourselves. We are also connecting with something profoundly human, since we all dream every night.

Dreaming is a universal language, which means that dreams have huge connective power in our fractured world. Why not create a tiny bit of healing change in the world by starting to ask the people in your life about their dreams? When we listen to the dreams of others, we see each other on the soul level. And what happens when somebody else sees you on the soul level? You light up inside! You shine. So, by sharing dreams, we bring more light into the world.

In this spirit, I'd like to share a recurring dream I have of diving deep into the ocean where everything is lit up and magical. I'm swimming powerfully into the depths, exploring and finding marvellous treasures. Then I rise back up to the surface and there are all these people sitting around on the rocks, and I'm so excited that I wave and call out:

"Hey—there's a whole other world down here! Come and see! Come and explore!"

This dream symbolises my enthusiasm for drawing people's attention to the magical and fascinating "other world" of dreams. I hope that with this book, the deep-sea-diving dreamer within me can encourage you to dive fearlessly into the magnificent world of lucid dreaming and discover its treasures for yourself.

I wish you happiness as you explore the "other world" beneath the waves.

APPENDIX I

Unique Lucidity
Programme Template

Here's where you combine your favourite practices for different sleeper /dreamer types from the fifteen Lucidity Programmes in chapter 4 to reflect your individual needs. Creating your own Unique Lucidity Programme personalises your lucid dream induction practice and fast-tracks you to wake up in your dreams.

Template

Sleeper/Dreamer Combination of Types

After taking the Lucidity Quiz in chapter 4, sum up the categories you most identify with in one phrase: "light sleeper, nightmare sufferer, good visualiser."

_____

_____

_____

Core Techniques

The fifteen Lucidity Programmes in chapter 4 recommend core practices for each sleeper/dreamer type. Navigate to the types that correspond with you, and choose a total of three practices that most appeal to you. Note the best time of day or night to practise them.

Practice X: _____

Timing: _____

Practice X: _____

Timing: _____

Practice X: _____

Timing: _____

Intent-Raising Practice

Choose one practice from this list: 7–10, 15, 19–25, or 39._____

_____

_____

Reality Checks

Pick three of your favourite reality checks from Practice 5 in chapter 2 or create your own—see *Practice 6: Invent Your Own Unique Reality Check*.

#1 _____

#2 _____

#3 _____

Pre-Sleep Routine

Create an inspiring routine (e.g., meditation + dream reliving + observe pre-sleep imagery, or dream incubation + pre-sleep visualisation to music). For ideas, see *Practice 4: Early Morning Meditation to Incubate a Lucid Dream* and *Practice 24: Create a Lucidity Ritual.* _____

_____

_____

Dream Journal

Do you plan to journal your dreams each day? Will you write the dreams down or sketch them? Will you underline moments where you nearly got lucid? How many dreams will you choose per week to vividly re-imagine as if you became lucid in them? Set yourself a couple of realistic goals.

Goal #1: _____

_____

Goal #2: _____

_____

Duration

Decide on a minimum length of time to follow this Lucidity Programme ... and stick to it if you can! _____

_____

_____

Appendix II

Examples of Unique Lucidity Programmes

I've picked out three common sleeper/dreamer combinations and have created Unique Lucidity Programmes for each of them so you can see how it works.

Unique Lucidity Programme 1

Sleeper/Dreamer Combination of Types
Heavy sleeper, low-recall dreamer, anxious/depressed dreamer.

Core Techniques
Practice 2: Power Up Your Dream Journal
Timing: Every morning

Practice 18: Surfing on the Edge of Sleep
Timing: Afternoon naps and at bedtime

Practice 10: Wake Up, Back to Bed
Timing: 5 hours into my night of sleep

Intent-Raising Practice

Practice 19: Sleep Under the Stars … or at Least in a Different Room.
Timing: 3 nights/week

Reality Checks

#1: The nose pinch
#2: The finger test
#3: Whenever someone smiles at me (even on TV)

Pre-Sleep Routine

Watch a YouTube video on lucid dream induction techniques (5 minutes), meditate to music (5 minutes), watch my pre-sleep imagery while repeating the mantra, "I am lucid."

Dream Journal

Goal #1: Write down every dream scrap I remember. Jot associations, underline moments when I nearly got lucid or could have seized the opportunity to do so!
Goal #2: Choose one dream per week to re-imagine as if I got lucid in it.

Duration

Two weeks, maintaining a steady habit of dream journaling and pre-sleep routine. Try sleeping somewhere different three nights each week to encourage a lighter sleep.

Unique Lucidity Programme 2

Sleeper/Dreamer Combination of Types

Light sleeper, high-recall dreamer, visual and imaginative thinker.

Core Techniques

Practice 23: Hone Your Strangeness Radar
Timing: Daytime

Practice 17: Shapeshifting
Timing: Pre-afternoon nap visualisation

Practice 36: Talk to Dream People, Objects, and Animals
Timing: Pre-bed visualisation

Intent-Raising Practice

Practice 15: Use Mini-Awakenings to Cement Your Intent to Get Lucid
Timing: Nighttime

Reality Checks

#1: The floatiness check
#2: The reading text test
#3: The tongue bite

Pre-Sleep Routine

Read a lucid dreaming book (5 minutes) + meditation (5 minutes) + visualisation

Dream Journal

Goal #1: Sketch core images for all dreams and use coloured pencils to represent emotions.
Goal #2: Vividly re-imagine four dreams per week, invent what I'd do if I were lucid in them.

Duration

One week for this programme, following it every day and every night and taking notes.

Unique Lucidity Programme 3

Sleeper/Dreamer Combination of Types

Nightmare sufferer, agitated sleeper (sleep paralysis episodes), and high-recall dreamer.

Core Techniques

Practice 24: Create a Lucidity Ritual
Timing: Before sleeping

Practice 55: The Lucid Imaging Nightmare Solution
Timing: After a nightmare

Practice 58: Sleep Paralysis Tricks
Timing: During a sleep paralysis episode

Intent-Raising Practice

Practice 39: Meditation for Clarity and Lucid Intent
Timing: Any time of day

Reality Checks

#1: Whenever I feel scared or uneasy
#2: The hands trick
#3: The light switch test

Pre-Sleep Routine

Relaxing bath + meditation (10 minutes) + dream reliving with positive changes to distressing elements + calming lucidity mantra: "I am lucid and perfectly safe."

Dream Journal

Goal #1: Focus on writing down as many dreams as possible to track themes and patterns, bearing in mind that recurring dreams are especially good for becoming lucid in.
Goal #2: Take the time to write out possible solutions and actions for dreams with distressing content. Play with the ideas from Practice 56: Ten Nightmare Options.

Duration

At least two weeks, and definitely until I've tried the Lucid Imaging Nightmare Solution straight after a nightmare, and the sleep paralysis tricks while actually in sleep paralysis.

Bibliography

Barrett, Deirdre. *The Committee of Sleep: How Artists, Scientists, and Athletes Use Dreams for Creative Problem-Solving—And How You Can Too.* New York, NY: Crown Publishers, 2001.

Bjorklund, Anna-Karin. *Dream Guidance: Interpret Your Dreams and Create the Life You Desire!* Newport Beach, CA: Crystal Souls, 2012.

Brown, David Jay. *Dreaming Wide Awake: Lucid Dreaming, Shamanic Healing, and Psychedelics.* Rochester, VT: Park Street Press, 2016.

Bulkeley, Kelly. "Lucid Dreaming and Ethical Reflection." Lucidity Letter 7, no. 1 (1988). https://journals.macewan.ca/lucidity/article/view/792/733.

Burk, Larry. "Warning Dreams Preceding the Diagnosis of Breast Cancer: A Survey of the Most Important Characteristics." *Explore: The Journal of Science and Healing.* 11(3), 2015, pp193–198.

Castaneda, Carlos. *Journey to Ixtlan*. New York, NY: Simon and Schuster, 1972.

Clark, Laurel. *Intuitive Dreaming*. Windyville, MO: SOM Publishing, 2012.

Dresler, Martin, et.al. "Dreamed Movement Elicits Activation in the Sensorimotor Cortex." *Current Biology* 21 (2011).

D'Urso, Beverly (Kedzierski Heart). "The Art of Dream Healing." Presentation at the International Association for the Study of Dreams (IASD) PsiberDreaming Conference. September, 2005. https://wedreamnow.info/

Epel, Naomi. *Writers Dreaming*. New York, NY: Vintage Books, 1994.

Erlacher, Daniel, Tadas Stumbrys, and Michael Schredl. "Frequency of Lucid Dreams and Lucid Dream Practice in German Athletes." *Imagination, Cognition and Personality* 31, no. 3 (January 2011): 237–246.

Garfield, Patricia. *Creative Dreaming*. New York, NY: Ballantine Books, 1976.

Hearne, Keith. *The Dream Machine: Lucid Dreams and How to Control Them*. Wellingborough, UK: Aquarian Press, 1990.

Hearne, Keith. "Lucid Dreams: An Electro-Physiological and Psychological Study." PhD diss., University of Liverpool, England, 1978.

Hoss, Robert and Robert Gongloff. *Dreams That Change Our Lives: A Publication of the International Association for the Study of Dreams*. Asheville, NC: Chiron Publications, 2017.

Hurd, Ryan. *Sleep Paralysis: A Guide to Hypnagogic Visions and Visitors of the Night*. Los Altos, CA: Hyena Press, 2010.

Hurd, Ryan and Kelly Bulkeley (eds). *Lucid Dreaming: New Perspectives on Consciousness in Sleep*. Santa Barbara, CA: Praeger, 2014.

Jay, Clare [Clare R. Johnson]. *Breathing in Colour*. London: Piatkus, 2009.

———. *Dreamrunner*. London: Piatkus, 2010.

Johnson, Clare R. "The Role of Lucid Dreaming in the Process of Creative Writing." PhD diss., University of Leeds, UK, 2007.

———. "Creative Lucid Dreaming: Waking Up in Dreams, in Life, and in Death." Paper presented at the Gateways of the Mind Conference, London, November 9–10, 2013.

Johnson, Clare R. *Llewellyn's Complete Book of Lucid Dreaming: A Comprehensive Guide to Promote Creativity, Overcome Sleep Disturbances & Enhance Health and Wellness.* Woodbury, MN: Llewellyn Worldwide, 2017.

———. "Celebrating 40 Years of Lucid Dream Exploration: A Dynamic Exploration of Lucid Dream Science, Therapy, Healing, Creativity, and the Dream Body." Event with Keith Hearne hosted by the Dream Research Institute, London, March 2015.

———. "Dream Magicians: Empower Children through Lucid Dreaming." In *Sleep Monsters and Superheroes: Empowering Children through Creative Dreamplay.* Edited by Clare R. Johnson and Jean M. Campbell. Santa Barbara, CA: Praeger, 2016.

———. *Dream Therapy: Dream Your Way to Health and Happiness.* London: Orion Spring, 2017.

———. "Lucid Dreaming and the Creative Writing Process." Paper presented at the Dream Writing Conference, University of Kent, October 15–16, 2005.

———. "Lucid Dreaming, Synaesthesia, and Sleep Disorders: Dreaming into Fiction." Paper presented at the 26th conference for the International Association for the Study of Dreams, Chicago, IL, June 26–30, 2009.

———. "Magic, Meditation, and the Void: Creative Dimensions of Lucid Dreaming." In *Lucid Dreaming: New Perspectives on Consciousness in Sleep.* Edited by Ryan Hurd and Kelly Bulkeley. Santa Barbara, CA: Praeger, 2014.

———. "Surfing the Rainbow: Fearless and Creative Out-of-Body Experiences." In *Consciousness Beyond the Body: Evidence and Reflections.* Edited by Dr. Alexander De Foe. Melbourne: Melbourne Centre for Exceptional Human Potential, 2016.

———. *Mindful Dreaming: Harness the Power of Lucid Dreaming for Happiness, Health, and Positive Change.* San Francisco, CA: Conari Press, 2018.

Johnson, Clare R., and Jean M. Campbell, eds. *Sleep Monsters and Superheroes: Empowering Children through Creative Dreamplay.* Santa Barbara, CA: Praeger, 2016.

Kellogg, Ed. "Lucid Dream Healing Experiences: Firsthand Accounts." Paper presented at the 16th Conference of the Association for the Study of Dreams in Santa Cruz, CA, July 6–10, 1999. www.asdreams.org/documents/1999_kellogg_lucid-healing.htm.

LaBerge, Stephen. *Lucid Dreaming: The Power of Being Awake & Aware in Your Dreams.* New York, NY: Ballantine Books, 1985.

LaMarca, Kristen, and Stephen LaBerge. "Pre-sleep Treatment with Galantamine Increases the Likelihood of Lucid Dreaming." Poster session presented June 25, 2012, at the 29th Annual Conference for the International Association for the Study of Dreams, Berkeley, CA.

Mallon, Brenda. *Dreams, Counselling and Healing.* Dublin: Newleaf, 2000.

Mascaro, Kimberly. *Extraordinary Dreams: Visions, Announcements and Premonitions Across Time and Place.* Jefferson, NC: McFarland, 2018.

Schädlich, Melanie. "Darts in Lucid Dreams: A Sleep Laboratory Study." Paper presented at the 33rd Annual Conference for the International Association for the Study of Dreams, Kerkrade, Netherlands, June 24–28, 2016.

Sparrow, Scott. *Lucid Dreaming: Dawning of the Clear Light.* Virginia Beach, VA: A.R.E. Press, 1976.

Stumbrys, Tadas and Daniel Erlacher. "Lucid Dreaming during NREM Sleep: Two Case Reports." *International Journal of Dream Research* 5, no. 2 (October 2012).

Waggoner, Robert. *Lucid Dreaming: Gateway to the Inner Self.* Needham, MA: Moment Point Press, 2009.

Wangyal, Tenzin Rinpoche. *The Tibetan Yogas of Dream and Sleep.* Ithaca, NY: Snow Lion Publications, 1998.

Resources

The International Association
for the Study of Dreams (IASD)

For readers who would like community support with their dreams or who want to deepen their exploration of dreamwork, I highly recommend becoming a member of IASD. This vibrant and friendly organisation brings dreamers together from all walks of life, creates fabulous dream conferences (easy-access online ones and others in global locations), and provides a wealth of expert dream advice, insight, and information through its member-exclusive *DreamTime* magazine and its academic journal, *Dreaming*. IASD is community-based, supportive, and fascinated by all aspects of dreaming. For me, it's like a second family. Find out more at www.asdreams.org.

Deep Lucid Dreaming

If you want to keep exploring lucid dreaming and go deeper, on my website you can browse articles on everything from lucid dream healing to nightmare solutions, pick up a free e-book on how to get and stay lucid, watch lucid dreaming videos, and contact me for advice (please understand that I get a lot of messages but I do my best to reply as fast as I can). I look forward to connecting with you! Visit www.DeepLucidDreaming.com.

My YouTube channel "Deep Lucid Dreaming Dr Clare Johnson" has plenty of short videos where I talk about different aspects of lucid dreaming: https://www.youtube.com/channel/UC3P-H6MiXL4oRQjocOrcxlw

You can also contact me on Twitter @LucidClare or come over to my Facebook pages: https://www.facebook.com/DeepLucidDreaming/ and https://www.facebook.com/LucidClare I'm on Instagram as clare_johnson_lucid _dreaming.

If you fancy the idea of exploring the healing, creative, wild, and spiritual aspects of lucidity in a small, relaxed group by the ocean, join me on one of my lucid dreaming retreats! For more information, see my website or write to deepluciddreaming@gmail.com.

Index